ECOTERRORISM

ECOTERRORISM

"Ignored and Unenforced Law"

PAUL E. TRUITT, DVM

To order additional copies of this book, contact:
Xlibris
1-888-795-4274
www.Xlibris.com
Orders@Xlibris.com
700561

CONTENTS

DEDICATION

I dedicate this book to a number of good souls that have shown me how family, friends, and neighbors should love one another.

My wife, Salvacion: Salvie is truly the best soul that I have ever met. She is a kind and cheerful giver. No matter how bad things seem, Salvie is always loving and kind.

My brother Joe: Joe is a year and a half younger than me. If not for Joe's brotherly love, I probably would not have survived my toughest times. Joe also rallied my other siblings to give their support. Thanks – Joe, Karen, Jerry, Linda and Brenda. Karen thank for providing Salvie and I with a roof over our heads!

My great-nephew Collin: Collin was a big, handsome, intelligent kid with a joy for life. A rare form of lung cancer took his life at the age of eleven. However, it never dimmed his spirit. Rather than feeling self-pity, Collin courageously told the doctors at the children's hospital that they could use him as a "guinea pig" - if it would help other kids in the future. Collin was literally the "spirit-child" for a non-profit organization, *Collin's Classic for Kids with Cancer* (now *Collin Cancer Fund for Children*), formed to help kids with terminal cancer. Collin has been an inspiration to me and many others.

Willis and David Goosaman: Willis and David were good neighbors. Willis and David were there when we needed them most. They cut and bailed hay for the Trust horses after SBT was forced out of business. They also cleaned out the barns and fixed my car. They refused payment for their kindness!

Ken Travis: Ken is another good neighbor, although we live hundreds of miles apart in different states. I had never met Ken until he offered to help. Ken has been like a brother. Ken is a retired government agent; therefore, he has encouraged me to hold the ecoterrorists' feet to the fire!!

INTRODUCTION

Mother Nature and Nature's Creator have a will, a plan, and a purpose for all of us. Since I was a little boy, I have had a fascination and love for animals of all kinds. At the age of 5, I started working with animals; my first chore was to feed baby calves each morning before school. I would lead a little Jersey nurse-cow out to the orchard where we kept the calves. Dairy cows give way too much milk for just one calf; therefore, as many as 4 calves would nurse at the same time. "Tiny" would contently stand there eating the grain that I would bring along for her. Once the calves had nursed her dry, I would lead her back to the barn.

For the next 60 years, the growth, health, safety and welfare of animals was my life's work. That was until a group of terrorists insanely decided that they had a right to interfere with my livelihood and prevent me from doing what I loved most. Consequently, my fate turned to fighting Evil; to put it another way, to stand up for what is good and just; especially, when it comes to animals and their caregivers.

My background has prepared me well for my fight again domestic terrorism. I grew up on an award winning livestock farm in Kentucky in a large Christian family. I developed courage, character, and respect for rules by playing sports. I graduated from Auburn University's School of Veterinary Medicine and practiced for 40 years and received hours of additional education each of those years. I was also a very successful Thoroughbred horse trainer, farm manager, and bloodstock agent with years of practical experience in the Thoroughbred industry.

During my mid-life crises, I went on a quest for *knowledge* and *wisdom*. I wanted to find out why people behave the way they do. I continued my education by studying psychology, philosophy, logic, education, business, comparative religion, and interpersonal communication. I became an avid reader of books written about these subjects.

In a quest for more knowledge, I also taught *"Human Health and Biology"* and *"Biology – The Nature of Life"* at the college level.

I am not a professional writer. I am a senior citizen whose life has been threatened; and, whose livelihood has been destroyed by a well-organized crime group masquerading as animal activists; a terroristic group that was aided and abetted by corrupt government agencies and race track officials.

During my lifetime, I worked for four different government agencies; thus, I become all too familiar with how some government officials abuse their power and authority. My first two government jobs were in KY; I surveyed farm crops for the Agriculture Stabilization and Conservation Service and I also worked for the KY Department of Transportation. I was still a shy teenager when I held those jobs; however, I had an innate need to do what was right. After I brought nonfeasance and malfeasance to their attention, my supervisors in KY promptly corrected the problems and went on with the business of running their agencies.

My next two government jobs were in Nashville, Tennessee. I was a lot older and wiser, but still had a need for to see that "wrongdoing" was corrected. However, my corrupt supervisors in Nashville took it *personal*. Instead of simply correcting the nonfeasance and malfeasance, they relentlessly and continuously retaliated with the malicious intent to destroy my career. They even threatened my life, if I did not stop "bucking the system" and go alone with the government wrongdoing.

As the founder and president of a 501 (c) (3) non-profit organization, Animal Health Safety and Welfare, Inc.; I studied non-profit organization management; and, I provided pro bono veterinary services for a number of legitimate non-profit organizations. Last but not least, I formed a mixed Charitable Trust to benefit financially troubled Thoroughbred owners and to educate and mentor those interested in a career in the Thoroughbred industry. I also designated three children's charities as beneficiaries of our Charitable Trust.

I was considered to be one of the best veterinary surgeons in Tennessee; and, for a period of time back in the 70's and 80's, I was highly successful as a bloodstock agent and Thoroughbred trainer. I have spent my entire life caring for the health, safety and welfare of animals of all kinds.

I have always had an altruistic side when it came to animals. While in practice, I never turned down a sick or injured animal for the lack of money; not even wild, homeless, or orphaned animals. When training or treating animals, I also put myself in their places.

Most recently, I worked as the general manager for the Thoroughbred Division of a proposed International School of Agriculture and Expo Center. After I was laid-off because of the lack of funding, my altruistic character came out again. I continued to volunteer 80+ hours per week to the non-profit organization to make sure that their horses were well taken care of. I also provided free veterinary services and brought feed, hay, supplies, and medicine out of my own pocket anytime they were needed.

CHAPTER 1

Good and Evil

Our Maker gave us "free will" – a choice between doing good and doing evil. During my early adult years, I evolved into a man with two distinct sides; that is, at one time I was influenced by both good and bad. As is often depicted in cartoons and movies, I had a little devil on one shoulder and a little angel on the other. As I fed the little angel on the right shoulder and starved the little devil on the left, I changed into a better man. Since that time, I have become filled with a "spirit" that naturally inspires me to do "good" – much like the spirit that I had in my childhood. Ironically, this spirit of doing what is right has cost me my livelihood and made me a continual target of corrupt government officials and a well-organized crime group; however, I have no regrets for my spiritual restoration. What is right in God's eyes is what really matters most!

I am a prime example of how our society and our Justice System are letting sociopaths - masked as public servants with noble causes - exploit their targeted victims for personal gain. However, I am not discouraged by this; because, any good philosopher, psychiatrist, or preacher will tell you – "the *evil in a thing will naturally destroy it*". And that Truth and Justice will always win. What Mankind does not "justify" in this life - the Divine Couple (Mother Nature and Nature's Creator) *will*.

For the last fifteen year or so, I have been casted into a continual battle against domestic terrorism and corrupt government. I have found that many government officials and religious leaders have a problem wrapping their minds around the fact that *terrorism* of any kind is not about politics or religion. Terrorists simply use religion and politics as covers to mask their despicable criminal activities. The fight against domestic or foreign terrorism is not a political or religious war; it is simply a fight between Good and Evil!!! My most recent battle has been against a politically charged "perverted non-profit organizations" (posing as animal rights activists). These groups who have turned "ecoterrorism" into a lucrative racket!!!

CHAPTER 2

Stand Up For What Is Right

During my mid-life crisis, I was spiritually born again. I decided not to straddle the fence any longer, if something was not alright with the "Spirit of God" within me, I was inspired to do something about it. After choosing the side of *Good*, I have continually found battles for what is right. This has made me a target for one sociopath after another.

When asked why I keep fighting these lopsided battles, the only way to answer my critics is that I believe fighting battles for *Good* is my fate in this life. If I don't stand up for what is right – who will? Many good people seem to think that just praying is enough these days. In my way of thinking, they are just spectators in the Game of Life and the battle between Good and Evil.

Much to my detriment most of my battles with evil forces were lost and left me standing alone. All that I worked for over 60 years has been taken away from me and my innocent beneficiaries. Even most of my family and friends wanted me to give up the fight. However, I have the spirit of a Thoroughbred horse; I lean into adversity; and, I don't have "quit" in me!

In my early years, I excelled in Basketball, Football, Baseball and Track & Field – and Academics. I was smart, big, strong, tall and fast. In one of my college courses, members of the class were tested to see what kind of animal they would be. Because of my size, athletic ability, intelligence and spirit, I was found to be most like a Thoroughbred horse. I was very proud of that and have always felt a spiritual connection with Thoroughbreds. The result of another psychological test revealed that my two biggest stressors were "insubordination" and "incompetence". As you will see later, my primary stressors played right into the hands of undercover ecoterrorists. Two of the undercover terrorists' devious objective was to specifically *cause me emotional duress; more specifically, "Do anything and everything that you can to 'piss' Dr. Truitt off"*.

Terrorists are nothing more than psychopaths – social parasites and/or predators!! Individuals with strong moral and ethical values will not tolerate the way psychopaths treat others. To my detriment, I have a history of recognizing and standing up to those who misuse their power and authority to unconscionably harm others.

As Fate seems to dictate, I keep finding myself in the mist of wrongdoers who are accustomed to having power and control over their perverted situations. My good nature and my need to do what is right motivate me to first ask the wrongdoers to correct the situation. In kinder and gentler times that often worked; however, some of those that I have confronted in today's society have an evil tendency to maliciously retaliation instead; and, in a textbook psychopathic ways!

Since terrorists are narcissistic psychopaths, they feel that no one has the right to questions their perverted power and authority, or interfere with their illegal or immoral schemes. *They aggressively hate*; hold in contempt; and, continuously retaliate against those who do not approve of their deceptive and coercive practices and affirm their despicable behavior.

For over fifteen years, my character and my career have been under relentless attacks by a continual gauntlet of evil-spirited wrongdoers that are legally classified as *domestic terrorists* and/or *ecoterrorists*. Their continuous economic, moral, and emotional duress has made it impossible for me to afford civil action against them. Although I have filed endless complaints against these corrupt individuals - federal, state, and local law enforcement have dismissed my claims simply as an ongoing "civil" feud between the terrorists and me; which has made it abundantly clear to me that the terrorists do in fact have covert government and political facilitators as they have openly and arrogantly claimed.

[*Note - As an early adult, what I considered my bad side would be considered absolutely normal today; maybe even admired!]

> [*Ecoterrorism is politically charged; therefore, it is often ignored by law enforcement – no matter how criminal and morally depraved it gets!]

I feel that I became the targeted victim of an extreme case of "mob monomania" - a psychosis characterized by thoughts confined to one idea. In my case, the mob monomania was to destroy my career and all my business relations no matter what it took. Even my life has been openly and covertly threated at times.

Many of the methods used by the terrorists to destroy careers and business relations are highly characteristic of psychopathic behavior; therefore, *it is important for the reader to understand how to recognize psychopathic behavior. Psychopathic behavior is often so camouflaged and so veiled that even the victims may have a hard time recognizing it until after most of the damage has been done. A similar phenomenon, known as "naïve prey syndrome", occurs in nature; the prey does not recognize the well-organized pack as predators until it is too late.*

In my case, my troubles started in Tennessee with a group of corrupt state government officials after I unknowingly exposed years of nonfeasance; which then quickly turned into malfeasance and retaliation. A few years later, I exposed another psychopathic in-group of corrupt metro government officials that targeted their honest, hardworking subordinates; and, pet store owners and their employees. All the wrongdoing in Nashville stemmed from perverted government officials not following state and federal laws and their own policies and rules.

Rather than simply correcting wrongdoing, corrupt government officials often choice to maliciously retaliate against anyone who exposes their wrongdoing; or, anyone who just simply brings it to the corrupt officials' attention as I did.

[*I have observed that framing and prosecuting "whistleblowers" is the most common form of retaliation used by corrupt government officials.]

Good and just laws (and the proper enforcement of good and just laws) are the only things that give us equal rights and make us equals. Rather than giving a righteous person equal protection under the law, an integral part of government corruption is to vilify, prosecute, and exploit innocent victims rather than guarding their rights – as they are obligated by law to do. This is what makes government corruption so despicable!

Government officials should be more like the referees of sporting events; required to enforce the rules so that all the players are treated equally and given a fair chance. Government officials can get away with wrongdoing; because, they don't have fans watching their calls.

[*Laws are the conscience of humanity; however, terrorists have no conscience and don't play by any rules.]

17

The perverted public servants in Nashville were not satisfied with just destroying my career as a veterinarian in Tennessee and causing me to lose my jobs, life-savings, home and farm; they followed me to Pennsylvania and continued their criminal conspiracy against me by jointing an international group of ecoterrorists that was very active in the Mid-Atlantic States. When they failed to completely destroy me in PA; they then followed me to KY. They have remained *insanely obsessed* with my every move; and, with destroying my life, my property, and my livelihood. They call it "job security".

[*Perverted govern officials and ecoterrorists believe - as corrupt leaders in ancient Greece and Rome believed - that if you are going to lie, steal and destroy lives, do it in a big and public way!!]

Back to the ecoterrorists – I do not want to mention many names in this book because I don't want to distract from the books educational and informational value; and, I still want to give any duped accomplices, law enforcement officials, or, benefactors another chance to enunciate their parts in the crimes committed.

Any self-respecting "duped" accomplices would in my opinion turn states evidence against these terrorists and stop the group from harming other targeted victims – both animal and human!!! However, they just don't seem to have the conscience, courage, or moral fiber to do so.

If the readers are interested – several members of the crime group incriminated themselves while trying to publically vilify me and to destroy all my business relations. *You be the judge.* A Facebook page was created just for that purpose: "Star Barn Thoroughbreds-Broodmares in Urgent Need of Placement"; Google Star Barn Thoroughbreds, if you want to verify my story. Furthermore, a few of coconspirators incriminated themselves in the June 2014 edition of the *Pennsylvania Equestrian*.

It is not hard to tell who the terrorists' leaders are; it is harder to tell which of the accomplices and/or benefactors were intentionally malicious; or, were *"expertly"* duped by their seasoned psychopathic leaders. Personally, I recognized them by their continuing tortuous actions and by their continuing criminal activities; by what they do and not by what they say; by the "fruits of their spirit".

One particular group of ecoterrorists claim to have undercover "people" working for: targeted Thoroughbred owners; law enforcement (State Police and FBI); Thoroughbred race tracks; majors TV stations, newspapers, and magazines; and, with nationally recognized animal rights groups, such as HSUS, ASPCA, and PETA. Many members of the crime group have publicized their involvement and/or it is a matter of public record. *Reality* and *the Truth* always shine a bright light on outrageous lies and evil deeds!! They are often the victim's only saving grace!

The terroristic group, that I am most familiar with, is a well-organized crime group which has developed an aggressive *mode of operation* specifically designed *to terrorize and exploit the Thoroughbred industry*. While operating under the charitable guise of rescuing Thoroughbred horses from slaughter, they have evolved into a misguided in-group with a perverted sense of authority and entitlement.

Common traits of domestic and foreign terrorists include: difficulty with compassion or empathy for their victims – animal or human *(any hint of compassion on their part is superficial and fake);* lack of shame or guilt; flatter those who admire and affirm them; detest and retaliate against those who do not admire them; abuse others rights without any consideration of the damages done; usurp legal authority; have no respect for the laws or rules of society; fabricate and exaggerate their achievements; degrade their victims (animal and human) while claiming to be experts at many things; feel no remorse or gratitude; see themselves as perfect; arrogant, often degrading others to inflate their own egos; obtains a false sense of superiority by using publicized contempt and *cyber-bullying* to minimize others; have an *insane sense of entitlement* to the property of targeted victims; exploit others without regard to the victim's feelings or rights; no boundaries; will destroy others without shame, guilt, or remorse, if the victim do not comply to their desires and demands; perceive themselves as better than others; perceive themselves as special; selfish; "unprincipled" – fraudulent, exploitative, deceptive, unscrupulous individuals; must be in control at any cost; *superficial charm*; grandiose sense of self-worth; *pathological liars*, but often project this and their other despicable traits onto their targeted victims; *master deceivers and manipulators*; fail to accept responsibility for their own actions; blame others, especially hardworking and honest individuals; perceive themselves as invincible; *magnets for codependents*; and, *prey on naïve, good, honest, trusting, and altruistic individuals.*

[*Perverted animal activists groups operate under the mask of non-profit organizations with noble causes; however, they often morph into well-organized crime groups; especially, when law enforcement ignores their crimes.]

You can judge a tree by the fruit that it bears. It is hard to find any real animal lovers on this conspiracy tree; or, people lovers as far as that go. Members of psychopathic in-groups simply are not capable of love; they have absolutely no respect for the rights of others – including animals.

Ecoterrorists are evil and insane; they would rather see their targeted owners' animals dead than to see the owners benefit from their animals. "You couldn't run a dead horse" is one of their veiled sayings.

[*Argumentum ad ignorantiam – terrorists prey on the ignorance of those who are trusting, altruistic, naïve, and honest.]

As the founder and operator of a truly altruistic charitable organization, Animal Health Safety and Welfare, Inc., with years of experience working with legitimate charitable animal rescue groups, I was able to recognize the perverted and predatory nature by which this group exploits Thoroughbred owners, breeders, and trainers - and the Thoroughbred industry in general. Furthermore, the alpha leader and "her people" often manipulates, exploits, and usurps the power and authority of race track officials; law enforcement agencies; and, the Justice System in order to carry out their despicable crime schemes.

Ecoterrorists have an aberrant indifference to the plight of both their animal and human victims. Under the protection of their undercover law enforcement officials and political backers, they lack due respect and obedience to the law; they feel that the rights of others, laws, and court orders are *"irrelevant"* - and do not apply to them.

Ecoterrorists are evil-doers; they are sociopaths. Leading psychologists estimated that as many as 30% of the world's population are sociopaths/psychopaths. That statistic may not include the many terrorists that often work "undercover" - as charitable organizations, religious groups, and political causes.

According to leading psychologists, the aftermath of dealing with psychopaths/terrorists and the recovery process can be a "long, slow and painful process" for their victims. Therefore, I want to share what I have learned about psychopaths/terrorists and psychopathic in-groups in general. A victim may be able to mitigate some of the damages by early recognition and by exposing the terrorists.

I am old school. I refer to terrorists as psychopaths rather than the more politically correct term – sociopaths or extremists. In reality, terrorists, ecoterrorists, sociopaths and psychopaths are basically the same.

*Warning: do not ignore or underestimate terrorists and terrorism of any kind; even if your family and friends think that you are being paranoid. Psychologists warn (and I have learned from experience) that if psychopaths/terrorists are not dead or incarcerated, they will continue to stalk and covertly target their victims – even after they have been found out. This tends to make the victim feel paranoid; although being painfully aware that you are being insanely targeted is not the same as being paranoid!!!!

The thing that I fear most is that this great country of ours is rapidly reaching a point of no return; that the apathy of its good citizens will continue to let psychopaths, terrorists, and corrupt government officials exploit our country - and the world!!! Once they have been recognized, the criminal motives of terrorists are so transparent!! There is no noble political or religious cause; terroristic acts are carried out simply for personal gain and sadistic pleasure. We are not in a political or religious war; we are in a fight between Good and Evil!! A fight that all good people of the world must courageously and honorably fight!!

CHAPTER 3

How to Recognize and Expose Terrorists

[*The most important thing that I can pass on to the reader is that naïve, honest, and trusting people need to know how to recognize and deal with psychopaths and terrorists.]

As a matter of fact, the problem of terrorism has become so great that this should be part of our formal education; especially, college prep. It would greatly benefit the good and just high school and college students most; since, many psychopaths fail to finish high school; their pathological tendencies usually develop by the time they turn 18 years of age. *Although terrorists generally run in packs, a psychopath/terrorist may also operate as a narcissistic lone wolf; as in school shootings.*

> *In treating any disease, you need a good history and a thorough evaluation of the signs for an accurate diagnosis!!! Terrorism is plaguing our world; terrorism is the most destructive and evil disease ever known to humanity. Terrorism is a social disease that needs to be eradicated!*
>
> *Terrorists are master liars and manipulators! You cannot judge terrorists by their superficial charm or by what they say; terrorists have to be judged by their aberrant behavior toward others!*

I have also found that many terrorists get extremely foul-mouthed; especially, when they are exposed!!! It is one of the most amazing transformations that I have ever observed; I describe the phenomenon as rapidly transforming from "charming" to "head-spinning ballistic" or "poltergeistic". It is like an abscess being lanced - all kinds of pus and corruption spew out!! A beautiful creature one moment – a venomous snake the next!!

The USA is no longer an "Ideal State". A tyrannical and oligarchical society like ours (masquerading as a democratic, materialistic, and/or capitalistic society) is the ideal breeding ground for greedy and psychopathic terrorists.

There is little difference between a successful and an unsuccessful psychopath spiritually speaking; all psychopaths are filled with an evil spirit. However, the successful psychopath may become the "Wolf of Wall Street"; a corrupt government official that has lots of power and authority; or, a tyrannical world leader; while unsuccessful psychopaths may be no more than social parasites or repeat criminal offenders. Terrorists like positions of power and authority. However, terrorists (except for undercover government officials and/or politicians - they have power and authority; and, they are social parasites and repeat criminal offenders) fit best into the repeat criminal offenders' category; they have mastered their signature crime schemes and often get away with their deceptive and coercive practices.

[*Note - Many of the following traits and behaviors of psychopaths are based on the works of two renowned psychologists, H. Cleckley and R. Hare, specifically - Harvey Cleckley's The Mask of Sanity and Robert D. Hare's Hare Psychopathy Checklist.]

This is not a new problem; it has been a problem since the biblical Adam and Eve and Cain and Able. Ancient societies were often ruled by psychopaths/terrorist/tyrants/murders. Although Mankind has evolved, we still have a major problem with psychopaths and terrorists. Just look at the many TV programs and movies that are based on real life stories that feature psychopaths – even the old Westerns are filled with psychopathic outlaws; and, the frequent news stories covering terrorism and corrupt government around the world. *In today's world, terroristic in-groups are often sophisticated; well-organized; and, masked as charitable, religious, and political causes.*

Because they are pathological liars *and* master manipulators, psychopaths depends on false perceptions to dupe others; whether it be for personal satisfaction, sex, power or money. They first and foremost rely on the "blind trust" of their victims; and, they prey on the gullibility of the general public - and the News Media.

To psychopaths and corrupt government officials - "perception is all that counts". Simply put - a psychopath has lost touch with Reality. Psychopathic behavior is often described as "humanity gone haywire". Terrorism is "politics and/or religion gone insane"!

Psychopathic in-groups learn how to masterfully create false impressions; and, how to continually reinforce the false impression by using a process called *"parroting"*. Once they have a false impression thoroughly engrained in the minds of their "duped" accomplices, benefactors, and targeted audience; they *build off the false perception; false perceptions go viral and rapidly spreads*!

For instance, domestic terrorists created and continually reinforced the insane lies that my license to practice veterinary medicine in TN had been revoked; and, that I had several counts of animal abuse on my record. After parroting these egregious lies on social media, they created and reinforced the insane lies that my former employer (Star Barn Thoroughbreds) sent horses to slaughter and starved and abused horses.

Then - they created and continuously reinforced, the false impression that I sent horses to slaughter and starved and abused horses. Then - they created and reinforced the despicable lies that my wife and my proposed new business venture (Starline Equestrian Center) sent horses to slaughter and starved and abused horses. The psychopathic terrorists that targeted me and my business relations caused their targeted audience to believe that these despicable lies were all absolutely true.

How insane were these despicable lies? Neither my wife nor my new business venture ever owned a horse or had a single horse under their care, custody or control. And at the time the despicable lies about me (sending horses to slaughter and starving and abusing horses) were fabricated, I had no horses under my care, custody, or control. My license to practice veterinary medicine has never been revoked; and, I have never been guilty of animal abuse.

Furthermore, *some of their undercover coconspirators that were* working for my former employer, Star Barn Thoroughbreds, *were legally culpable* for health and safety of the very horses that the crime group claimed were being starved and abused.

It does not stop there; years after the ecoterrorists had force SBT out of business, they were still blaming SBT for the deaths of horses that undercover members of their crime groups had stolen from another business entity - my Charitable Trust; and, a number of perverted charities that are privately ran by members of the crime group were still soliciting money to train and care for the stolen horses!!!!

Psychopathic ecoterrorists cannot comprehend the fact that animals and other human beings have rights. These in-groups first have a tendency toward undercover *passive aggression*. They are cowards that use undercover saboteurs ("undercover investigators" as they like to call them) to exploit their victims, which also allows them to distort the truth and to quietly get away with their undercover criminal activities.

Terrorists do not *come out from hiding* until their victims have been *imploded* to such an extent that the psychopathic terrorists are 99.9% sure that the victims cannot fight back; and, they feel that they can "finish" the victims off. Often the victims are not aware that they have been targeted until after the *"bomb goes off"!*

[*Note: Even though terrorists will often use high-school dropouts as undercover accomplices, I would like to make it clear that I don't believe that all high-school dropouts are psychopaths. Or that all psychopaths are high-school dropouts. I know some very good and talented and successful high school dropouts. I also know some well-educated people that seem to exhibit psychopathic traits.]

According to leading psychologists, many psychopaths are in fact developmentally stuck in their early years, still fighting the battles of authority and parental control over them!

Psychopaths/terrorists must get their way or they will make trouble!

Psychopaths also tend to gravitate toward positions of power; power and recognition give them the satisfaction they crave; ultimately, they want total control over their victims, even if it means killing the targeted victims (animals or human beings).

Case in point: When my former employer Star Barn Thoroughbreds, refused to turn two mares over to the psychopathic in-group. The ecoterrorists *(knowing that it would leave their young foals orphaned)* allegedly brought in their big league animal rights activists (PETA, HSUS, and ASPCA) and threatened to have Dr. Barr prosecuted for animal cruelty - *if he did not have the mares immediately destroyed*!!! This was despicable; I knew at this point that we were not dealing with legitimate animal lovers; I knew that we were dealing with some *deeply disturbed* individuals!!

When I sent complaints to the FBI, the response that I got was: "be sure to notify your family and friends of what is going on." What I really heard them say was: "we are not going to do a damned thing; but, be sure to notify your family and friends of what is going on, so we will know who to look for if they kill you". I also heard the FBI said that "killing and stealing Thoroughbred horses is a 'civil' matter"; and, you need to get a civil lawyer."

Psychopaths/terrorists have an insane sense of entitlement which motivates them to fabricate elaborate schemes of deception that will cause pain and loss to the intended victims; and, allow them to freely take away the things that the victims values most.

In the support of the scientific observations made by leading psychologists stating that psychopaths are often uneducated; many members of psychopathic in-groups have a difficult time with spelling and grammar. Check out some of their posts on their Facebook page - "Star Barn Thoroughbreds – Broodmares in Urgent Need of Placement".

In agreement with my favorite philosopher, Socrates – some members of psychopathic in-groups really seem "ignorant". Knowledge of the Truth seems to the best way to fight evil and injustice!

Although psychopaths may not be well-educated, they are always "experts at everything" in their own twisted minds. And ecoterrorists have come up with deviant ways to harm and kill animals; ways that go undetected and uninvestigated; and, reflect badly on the targeted owners.

Psychopaths want no interference with their control or dominance. Those that recognize and expose a psychopath/terrorist can expect unending retaliation. There is no known treatment for a psychopath/terrorist, so the only deterrent is incarceration - or death. In fact, psychotherapy is exploited by psychopaths/terrorists to sharpen their deviant talents and skills.

> *"Lying, deceiving, and manipulation are natural talents for psychopaths... When caught in a lie or challenged with the truth, they are seldom perplexed or embarrassed -- they simply change their stories or attempt to rework the facts so that they appear to be consistent with the lie. The results are a series of contradictory statements and a thoroughly confused listener." – R. Hare*

> *[*Death; divine judgment; and, eternal damnation of evil souls are the only ways that I see that will eliminate psychopaths, terrorists, murderers and tyrants from the world!]*

Psychopaths are commonly known to be cruel to animals. *Ecoterrorists are "experts at aggravated animal cruelty"*; they find ways to kill and harm animals that will go undetected. Contrary to this common viewpoint, many unexposed ecoterrorists are perceived as being animals lovers; however, the fact is *they have no capacity to love animals or other humans;* in fact, the animals and people they pretend to love are mere objects of their twisted crime schemes.

Psychopaths/terrorists have an extreme sense of entitlement; the insane attitude that they have a perfectly logical right to take whatever they desire. If you stand in the way of their desires or demands, or violate one of their rules, they insanely feel they are entitled to punish you in any manner they see fit!

For instance, if you participate in Thoroughbred breeding or racing, some insane anti-racing activists feel that they are entitled, justified, and have the right to punish you and deprive you of your horses in any way that they see fit – anything that will prevent you from participating in the Thoroughbred industry.

In reality, the *"anti-racing persona"* is just a smoke screen; *the real motive is personal gain in the form of fraudulently solicited donations and high-quality Thoroughbred horses that become free for the taking once the owner has been vilified, falsely prosecuted, put out of business, and/or permanently disabled.*

Terrorists are extremely hostile toward criticism and often react with anger or rage when their insane behavior is questioned. A psychopath/terrorist will not tolerate not getting their way. Terrorists usually *work on* their targeted victims by first constantly *degrading and/or vilifying* them. This is an integral part of all their crime schemes! Terrorists' insane sense of entitlement motivates them to fabricate outrageous schemes of deception designed to destroy the lives of those they *actively hate.* Successful terrorists use physical, economic, emotional, and moral duress to weaken and to cause permanent damage to their victims.

In order to control a target completely, the terrorists must cut off the victim's economic, emotional, moral, and legal support: get them fired; steal or destroy their property; interfere with their business relations; threaten or harm their family and friends; frame the victim for allegedly breaking the law; harming or killing the target's animals; etc.

If successful in framing their victims, psychopaths/terrorists gain great satisfaction from seeing their innocent victims wrongfully deprived of their dignity; their jobs; their property; and, especially their freedom (in cases where they are able to get the targeted victim incarcerated for something they didn't do).

Once the victims are isolated and alone, without support, the terrorists' control over them can increase - and the victim can be easily destroyed! Ecoterrorists will try to destroy the mental health of their victims and/or to cause others to perceive their victims as being mentally ill. *They project their traits onto the victim.* The victim is often perceived as paranoid; especially, by those who cannot believe that other human beings would do such evil things to the victim or the victim's animals.

A favored technique of terroristic in-groups is to vilify the victim by parroting false accusations and/or questioning the victim's honesty, integrity, trustworthiness, motives, character, competence, skills, sanity, and judgment. This style of manipulation is also well-suited for politics and perverted religious beliefs.

One of the most obvious signs of terrorism is the ease with which terrorists break rules. Rules and court orders are "irrelevant" to them! They will fabricate evidence; create false impressions; reinforce their outrageous lies; commit perjury; and, commit fraud on the court without any *sense* of having done anything wrong.

Psychopaths/terrorists typically are habitual criminals who often get away with their crimes. As an example, arsonists often start fires and then put them out so others will perceive them as heroes. Ecoterrorists often operate in the same manner; they will harm animals to coerce, terrorize, and falsely prosecute their targeted owners; while claiming to have heroically *"rescued"* the harmed animals from the maliciously vilified and framed owners.

Despite their evil-doing, psychopaths/terrorists are very narcissistic and see themselves as the center of the universe; as superior human beings who are justified in living according to their own rules.

Psychopaths/terrorists are addicted to power and control. If someone should actually attempt to "question" their power and control, they will react to some extent to harm the person and/or something dear to them. My favorite horses seemed to be the first to be harmed and/or killed. If I gave a horse a high evaluation, it was as if I doomed them to death or destruction. Jockey's Dream - the beautiful stallion on the cover of the book - was dear to me. He was 16.3 hands tall with a huge, muscular, and classy body; and, an exceptionally beautiful head, which I greatly admired. Knowing the brutal insanity of terrorists, I am not surprised that he was stolen and *"beheaded"*!!!

Psychopaths/terrorists will batter their victims; physically, psychologically, economically, prosecutorally, socially, and especially professionally. Most terrorists will not stop until they have permanently destroyed their targeted victims and taken everything that the victims values.

In my case, the psychopathic ecoterrorists targets Thoroughbred breeders, owners, veterinarians, farm managers, and trainers. (Being a well-educated professional that stands up for what is right made me even more of a target.) Ecoterrorists will sabotage a Thoroughbred operation by recruiting and using undercover employees ("investigators"). Covert members of the crime group start false and malicious rumors; damage property; abuse and kill horses; steal feed, medications, and supplies; publish *altered* and unflattering pictures of the owner's horses; file false reports of animal abuse against the owner; and then take horses by theft by deception, coercion, and/or extortion.

> [*"Parasitically bleeding other people of their possessions, savings, and dignity; aggressively doing and taking what they want; shamefully neglecting the physical and emotional welfare of the victims and their families; and so forth." - R. Hare*]

Instead of being justly prosecuted for their wrongdoing, their "false facade" (masquerading as animal rights activists) gives ecoterrorists the opportunity to be the "heroes" as they leap to the aid of the falsely perceived "starved and abused" horses; and, to thoroughly enjoy what their fabricated and "shocking" press stories precipitate in the way of ill-gotten donations!

Last, but not least, ecoterrorists often get legal control of the targeted owners' valuable Thoroughbreds under the tainted color of the law - by duping law enforcement and by usurping the authority of a duped and/or corrupt justice system. They also gain perverted pleasure from the pain that they cause the owners by framing the owners or trainers and depriving them of beloved animals - and their dignity – and even their health.

Psychopaths/terrorists get a sadistic pleasure by causing others pain! Some of the most common means are to steal or destroy something of value to their victim; to vilify the victim; and, to harm something or someone the victim loves. In the psychopath's mind, this is justified because the victim crossed them, did not give them what they wanted, or rejected them.

Terrorists often vilify their targets by projecting their own despicable traits onto their targeted victims; must like the terrorist groups, Al Qaeda and ISIS, portray Muslims and Christians who oppose their perverted causes as ungodly "infidels".

CHAPTER 4

Flawed Democratic Treatment

The covert strength (their masks of sanity) of ecoterrorists is also their Achilles heel. Once they have been spotted, identified, understood, and no longer have the power to deceive; once knowledge and truth enters the game, they are exposed, and have no more ability to "con" the other players or "dupe" their accomplices and donors. However, unprosecuted masterminds move on to the next target; even though, *they will never stop covertly targeting the ones who expose them.* And, if someone has to take the fail, duped accomplices are "thrown under the bus".

The thing that domestic terrorists fears most is public exposure. This pulls back the veil that they have been hiding behind; thus, greatly cutting down on the number of unsuspecting future targets. However, many successful ecoterrorists are able to manipulate the media in order to cause even more damage to their targets. This tactic is often used by corrupt government officials to get back at whistleblowers. I was simply told that I could, or would, be killed or maimed, if I went public with my supervisors' wrongdoing. Personally, I feel like I was placed on some kind of corrupt government "blacklist" – simply for doing what was right.

What is acceptable, or unacceptable, varies widely across cultures. Telling lies and cheating is perceived as impolite but acceptable in our democratic society (good and bad are basically treated as equals). Perjury and fraud on the Court are common place; but rarely prosecuted. I was told by the DA in Nashville that it would grid-lock the Justice System, if he tried to prosecute everyone who lied in legal proceedings.

Personally, I think it would be highly effective in taking away some of the deceptive power of psychopaths. Psychopaths believe that *"there is power and control in a lie." By not playing by the rules, psychopathic terrorists have a big advantage!*

The way our democratic, capitalistic, and materialistic society deals with psychopathic behavior has a lot of flaws; flaws that will continue to weaken our society and may even destroy it. Psychopaths represent humanity gone haywire.

The corrupt government officials in Nashville went to the extreme of oppressing and perverting free speech by enforcing a new "policy" that no one could communicate with the News Media without first getting the approval of their supervisors (their corrupt supervisors). I was also forbidden to attend public meetings.

Tennessee is #3 on the list of *"The 10 most corrupt states in the U.S."- written by Chris Matthew* in June 10, 2014. Since the rankings were based on the *number of convictions*, either TN or PA could easily be #1 - because both states ignore and fail to prosecute government corruption and corrupt organizations.

In a nutshell - if someone tells the truth and it is detrimental to a corrupt government official with power and authority, the corrupt official will turn on the truthful person in a twisted way and prosecute the truth-teller.

Truth-tellers are at risk in a society corrupted by psychopaths, terrorists, and corrupt government officials!

[*Case in point - Socrates was *executed* for saying that corruption was going to destroy the Roman Empire; and, Galileo was *prosecuted* and given a life sentence by the Roman Catholic Church for believing that the Earth rotates around the Sun!]

Politically charged psychopathic in-groups also know how to capitalize on "free speech"; "free speech" that is perverted to deceive and dupe the public. In our society, "free speech" (even though it may be nothing more than a pack of egregious lies) is valued far more than the victims' rights.

In our society, perverted "speech" in the form of insane lies is "freely" used to: vilify and prosecute victims; take the victims' property; deprive the victims of their happiness; deprive the victims of their right to work in their chosen professions; and, deprive the victims' of their rights to dignity and privacy. I say these things because I love my country and what it stand for; and, because I do not want to see psychopaths, terrorists, tyrants, and corrupt government official destroy it.

The past behavior of a society is often exploited by psychopaths/terrorists and used to predict the future behavior of that society; especially, a tyrannical and oligarchical society masquerading as a healthy democracy. As most victims of psychopathic in-groups will find, our Justice System is not willing to hold a politically charged crime groups accountable. Most criminal complaints are ignored or dismissed as *civil* matters; treated as disputes or ongoing feuds *between the victims and the psychopaths/terrorists;* thus, leaving the battered victims to fight an extremely inequitable civil battle.

[*Simply put, there is no cure for psychopathic social parasites; they must be removed from society or they will destroy it by targeting one good and just citizen at a time!!!!!]

In order to reduce psychopathic behavior in a society and in government, the society MUST establish a "reputation" for detecting master liars and deceivers (psychopaths/terrorists) - and for bringing them to justice. In other words; an Ideal State must establish a successful strategy to prosecute antisocial and criminal behavior and not ignore it.

It seems that in our society – professional athletes are tried by public opinion and punished for immoral behavior. Athletes who blatantly break the rules certainly don't get to stay in the game. If they lie to the public, even their esteem is taken away. Maybe that is why sports are so popular and our government gets such bad approval ratings. Sports are played for the fans; the government should be run for the benefit of its good and just citizens.

What consequences do liars and cheaters in our society and government suffer? Usually none!! In fact, in nearly every case, they are rewarded handsomely with those things of value to psychopathic terrorists - power, sex, money, promotions to positions of authority, winning elections, and their cut of the victim's (the citizen's) exploited goods. If anyone thinks that a psychopath is shamed by public exposure, think again! They have no conscience! They feel no shame or remorse!!! Psychopathic behavior is often amplified by a perverted politically backed in-group.

Our society often views domestic terrorists as political or religious activists with noble causes; when in fact, they are simply evil-spirited social parasites, predators, and criminals.

A society's backbone is its moral values and work ethics. Too often those who are in positions of authority have gotten there by taking the moral low-road. Psychopathic undercover saboteurs pervert work ethics and loyalty to their employers into theft and betrayal!

History demonstrates that uninhibited *greed and corruption* is always the most profitable strategy possible for personal gain!! The obvious solution would be a world in which terrorists - in government or in society - would be at the very least punished for their obvious criminal behavior.

In a society that accepts the moral low-road; domestic terrorists have an *extreme advantage* over the good, honest, trusting, altruistic members of the society. If I had not experienced it firsthand and for such a long time (the last fifteen years), I might also be reluctant to believe how corrupt our society and our government have gotten.

CHAPTER 5

Universal Human Rights

Terrorists, ecoterrorists, domestic terrorists, psychopaths, tyrants, and/or corrupt government officials - they are all the same. These narcissistic people insanely and inhumanely believe that their perverted political positions and/or religious beliefs give them the right and justification to deprive their targeted victims of their livelihood; to interfere with their economic relations; to destroy or take private property; and, to deprive their victims of their hopes, dreams, health, and anything else that is near-and-dear to their targeted victims; they do not feel that others have rights – not even the right to life. Those who could and should protect the victim do nothing!

The entire world has to reject the notion that "terrorists are merely religious and/or political activists"; when in reality, they are nothing more that psychopathic criminals – inhumane beings who in reality have forfeited their human rights by insanely infringing on the rights of other!

Socrates said that the biggest problem with a "democracy" is that it treats good and evil as having equal rights; and, that a democracy will eventually decay and decline into a society ruled by rich tyrants. *(Are we there yet?)* In an Ideal State, evildoing should *not* be tolerated; ignored; or, admired. In an Ideal State criminals forfeit their rights. The Ideal State must guard the rights of its good and just citizens; it should not protect the evil and unjust citizens to the detriment of its good and just citizen.

For a democracy to survive, it must guard against giving tyrants, psychopaths, and/or terrorists power and authority. Above all, an "Ideal State" must not allow tyrants to infringe on the rights of or exploit its good citizens; and, it must not let its just guardians (good and hardworking

---

34

government employees) to be deprived of their jobs - simply because they did what was right.

A democracy often declines into a society that tolerates and ignores politically motivated crimes; thus, giving psychopathic terrorists an extremely unfair advantage!

After fighting corrupt government officials in TN and PA for the last fifteen years, I have come to realizes that most of my rights have been violated by domestic terrorists; and, then ignored by law enforcement. Because of government corruption, those two states ignore organized crime.

Human rights are essential; however, we are living in a society that often violates and ignores human rights. Terroristic objectives masked as noble political or religious causes are often ignored (compounded) by law enforce and the Justice System. Politically charged psychopathic crime groups masked as non-profit organizations are given a *"license" to oppress and exploit individuals* that stand up for what is good and just.

Human Rights should not be violated or ignored, anywhere in the world. Government corruption is the evil that will destroys a society. Under the law, those that violate or ignore the rights of others should automatically forfeit their rights!!!! That should apply to terrorists of all kinds, perverted tax-exempt organizations, and corrupt government officials. These corrupt groups in particular seem to be exempt from prosecution!

Ecoterrorists specialize in turning the dreams of legitimate animal lovers into nightmares. Hiding behind the shield of perverted charitable organizations and corrupt government agencies, well-orchestrated crime groups are given *a "license" to vilify an animal owner and to kill, harm and steal the owner's targeted animals - all under the prevented pretense of official right.*

Sociopathic terrorists twist the right of *freedom of speech* to "trump" *defamation.* Duped and/or corrupt law enforcement ignores and compounds the activities of domestic terrorists. Terrorism of all kinds dishonors all of Mankind!!!!

Laws and rules are the collective conscience of a society. Because psychopathic terrorists have no conscience, they have a total lack of respect for the rules and laws. This is extremely apparent!

Corrupt political organizations pervert laws to vilify and falsely prosecute those that oppose their wrongdoing. In reality, the USA is no longer a true democracy; it is controlled by the rich and greedy that prey the naivety of the voters; and, "masked" tyrants that are given power and authority.

Perverted non-profit organizations and perverted political in-groups maliciously destroy their targets' lives; including, their livelihood, health, dignity, and happiness. *Many corrupt government agencies aid and abet crime groups by wrongfully seizing property and falsely prosecuting the targeted victims.*

As defined by PA statutes – ecoterrorism was a common practice in Nashville; ecoterrorism is a lucrative racket in PA that is ignored. Aided by corrupt law enforcement officers, the ecoterrorists in PA did and took whatever they please.

For example - in my case, the ecoterrorists in PA, despicably took by theft by deception 17 healthy Thoroughbred weanlings; and, then without a spark of dignity, they substituted several dead, sick and starved horses for nine of the healthy horses in an attempt to frame my former boss and/or me; so that they could keep all 17 of the valuable healthy animals.

Court orders to return the horses were "irrelevant". In contempt of a court order, members of this evil group wrongfully disposed of the Trust's healthy weanlings by using them as secret rewards. The crime group extorted all 17 horses by threatening prosecution and/or $90,000 in restitution; if, I forced them to honor the Court Order!

Then when I would not turn over the documents necessary to register several stolen horses with the Jockey Club, the ecoterrorists insanely killed many of the horses; then used their deaths, dead carcasses, bones, and "headless bodies" to create more *"shock value"* - *the primary tool which perverted non-profit groups despicably use to raise donations.*

> *"You couldn't run (or breed or make any money off) a dead horse"* is *their arrogant and perverted motto!*

Ecoterrorism statutes in Pennsylvania are meant to protect the rights of animals and the human rights of their owners. Human rights are meant: to fight the *"evils"* that perverted human beings intentionally inflict on others to exploit them; to secure a person's right to make a living at their chosen profession; and, to protect a person's right to own, enjoy, and benefit from their property.

Perverted animal rights activists despicably target and exploit veterinarians, Thoroughbred owners, breeders, and trainers primarily for personal gain and the sick pleasure they experience when they destroy lives – animals and humans.

I believe that animals, like humans, have a soul. Animal rights are meant to protect animals from being stolen, killed, maimed, starved, and abused. Ironically and despicably, ecoterrorists use undercover vandals (which they like to call undercover investigators and/or authorities) to carry out these despicable acts - *all under the perverted pretense of protecting the animals' rights.*

In reality, their real objectives are to falsely accuse and frame their loving owners; to steal the animals from the owners under the perverted pretense of official right; and, to fraudulently raise money to allegedly care for wrongfully seized and stolen animals.

Outrageously, even long after valuable and beloved animals were stolen, killed, and/or wrongfully disposed of, these *degenerates* continue to fraudulently soliciting donations to care for the dead and stolen horses; horses that they egregiously misrepresented as *"rescued"*! Furthermore, the stolen property was (and will always be) private Trust property that I was desperately trying to safeguard for the beneficiaries of our Charitable Trust; property that would have benefited critically ill children!!

I grew up on an award winning livestock farm in KY. I am a retired veterinarian who has spent his entire life carrying for the health, safety, and welfare of animals of all kinds. Yet - I was targeted by a well-organized group of psychopathic ecoterrorists, which was aided and abetted by a number of apathetic and/or corrupt government agencies.

To eliminate their competition, domestic terrorists (who operate perverted charities) also target legitimate charitable organizations. In my case, they despicably destroyed Agrarian Country, a 501 (c) (3) non-profit organization that had a lot of good things planned for the local community and the Commonwealth of Pennsylvania; including, an International School of Agriculture. After sabotaging Agrarian Country, they took by death, coercion, theft by deception, and extortion over 70 targeted Thoroughbred horses which belong to the innocent beneficiaries of our private Charitable Trust.

> *The terrorists maliciously and insanely deprived me of my right to work as a veterinarian; and then, my rights to own, breed, and train Thoroughbred horses.* [Ecoterrorism per se]

The psychopathic veiled joke of the ecoterrorists is - *"you couldn't run a dead horse"*. Several of our high-quality Thoroughbreds have died because of these perverted individuals. I fear that many more may have been killed simply to insanely prevent *me* from making any money off them; *it was as if the rights of the beneficiaries of the Trust were of no concern to the terrorists.* Of course, the real motive was to create "shock value" needed to fraudulently raise donations for the leaders of the groups.

The rights of innocent victims are of no concern to terrorists; they insanely feel that the collateral damage is justified; because, they are insanely entitled to destroy their targeted enemies!

The International Covenant on Economic, Social and Cultural Rights (ICESCR) emphases how important the *"right to work"* is to individual freedoms and to economic, social, and cultural development of all nations. I wish that the Justice Systems of Tennessee, Pennsylvania, and the United States felt the same.

I received no protection from the US Government or from the local and state authorities when domestic terrorists maliciously deprived me of my livelihood; most of my private property; and, the property that I was holding in Trust. *My complaints were ignored on all levels of the Justice System.*

Article 6 of the International Covenant states that the right to work, includes the *right of everyone* to the opportunity **to gain his living by work which he** *freely chooses or accepts,* and that States will take appropriate steps to safeguard this right. And that *the States must safeguard these fundamental political and economic freedoms of the individual. This is not how the corrupt governments of TN and PA felt; they felt it was a "civil" matter between me and the terrorists; as did Eric Holder, U.S. Attorney General.*

The *"right to work"* is a human right to engage in meaningful and productive employment and absolutely *no one* has the right to prevent a person from doing so. *"Everyone* **has the** *right to work,* **to a** *free choice of* **employment, to** *just and favorable conditions of work,* **and to** *protection against unemployment."*

Corrupt government officials and perverted animal activists feel that because of their tyrannical political views, they are entitled to interfere with the rights of those who choose to make a living participating in legal activities involving animals and that they have an official right to deprive owners of their beloved animals.

> *Ecoterrorists don't have a spark of honor or dignity; so they try to deprive their victims of these virtues. Even animals have more self-esteem, honor, and dignity than these evil inhumane beings.*

All that said - under close scrutiny the deceptive and coercive practices of terrorists and corrupt government employees are motivated primarily by greed and envy (personal gain); the perverted causes are only used as a manipulative *"cover"*. Ecoterrorists feel no guilt or shame when it comes to destroying the lives of animals or humans for selfish gain.

The very essence of the laws against ecoterrorism is meant to protect the very basic universal human right to work; and, the rights to own, enjoy, and benefit from agriculture related property.

Domestic terrorists are shameless and lack the human ability to feel guilt. Even their duped accomplices do not have a spark of courage or honor; after aiding and abetting the terrorists and the truth comes to light, they are too ashamed and cowardly to come forward to aid the damaged victims. Ironically, history shows that tyrants usually turn on and destroy their duped accomplices after their usefulness has run its course!

Another **Universal and Inalienable Human Right** is the *"right to property"* - and the right to *"equal protection"* of that private property. However, the right to property is not absolute and states have a wide degree of discretion to limit the rights. These *defects* in the laws have given perverted animal activists and corrupt government agencies *a "license to steal and kill animals" belonging to targeted owners under the perverted pretense of official right. The corrupt govern officials in Nashville targeted pet stores; the ecoterrorists in PA targeted valuable Thoroughbreds.*

The American Convention on Human Rights (ACHR) recognizes the right to protection of property, including **the right to *"just compensation"*.** The ACHR also prohibits exploitation. **Every person has the right to own private property; property that is necessary to make a living and to the dignity of the individual.**

> *I loved my Thoroughbred horses and they loved me; yet law enforcement allowed ecoterrorists from all over the country to vilify me and to wrongfully deprive me of my beloved horses.*

Everyone has the right to the use and enjoyment of their property – and to just compensations. This is as old as Moses:

> *"Thou shalt not covet thy neighbour's house; thou shalt not covet thy neighbour's wife, or his manservant, or his maidservant, or his ox, or his ass, or anything that is thy neighbour's."*

I assume that this basic law of morality covers one's Thoroughbred horses and related property.

No one shall be deprived of his property. Any form of exploitation of man by man is prohibited by law. Exploitation is in the evil heart-and-soul of terrorism of any kind. Often masked as perverted charities, ecoterrorists use elaborate crime schemes to exploit their targeted victims.

One integral part of terroristic crime scheme is to cause and use economic duress and other well-orchestrated "misfortunes" to takes advantage of their targets.

Another ploy used by psychopathic in-groups is to use their *perverted* *"freedom of expression"* to vilify their targets and to falsely prosecute their victims. They use their social media networks to parrot fabricated lies until the despicable falsehoods are *"perceived"* as the truth and the targeted victim is held in contempt and hatred.

Masked as noble causes, the terroristic crime schemes are motivated by hatred, greed, and envy - solely for personal gains and perverted pleasure. *Continual harassment and stalking* meant to cause overwhelming emotional distress is also an integral part of terroristic crime schemes.

That brings up another basic human right - the **"right to health"**; the right to a standard of living adequate for the **health and well-being** of himself and his family; including, food, clothing, housing, medical care, necessary social services, and the right to security in the event of unemployment, sickness, disability, widowhood, old age, or the *lack of a livelihood caused by circumstances beyond his control;* especially, circumstances insanely brought on by an evil political in-groups or corrupt government officials.

Ecoterrorists try to deprive their victims of their livelihood and dignity; and, they covertly harm and threaten the targets property and beloved animals, while illegally seizing healthy animals and attempting to frame and prosecute the owner for animal cruelty.

I can only adequately describe the behavior of domestic and foreign terrorists as "pure evil"!!!!!!!!!!!!

The US Attorney General, the State *Attorney General,* and *District Attorneys* all have the power and *duty* to enforce criminal law; especially, when the crime scheme transverses a number of states.

Legal rights *must* be protected; and, those who have infringed on another's legal rights must be prosecuted. Our rights must be protected by *court orders* or *injunctions* prohibiting the other person or persons from infringing our rights; and, by the awarding of restitution to compensate the holders of the rights. *Good laws and the enforcement of the laws are what make all human beings equal.*

CHAPTER 6

Facts of Law & Ecoterrorism Defined

I greatly admire and appreciate all the courageous and honorable people who serve God, Mother Nature and Humanity for the common good of all!! However, these brave souls are often quietly disarmed and falsely prosecuted by corrupted government in-groups who will do anything to keep their power and authority!

[*Orders of the Court are "irrelevant" to ecoterrorists. Orders of the Courts do nothing more than give a psychopath an adrenalin rush!* They get great satisfaction out of duping the courts. Ecoterrorists play by no rules; all a psychopathic in-group has to do is to get their members to file false affidavits and bear false witness in Court when needed to cover-up wrongdoing; or, to falsely prosecute a targeted victim – this is exciting to them!!]

> *I have not fully figured out why the state governments of Tennessee and Pennsylvania and the US Government have chosen to repress my complaints and/or to add insult to injury by using official oppression to discourage me from seeking justice. However, the answer seems to be politically motivated in some way; probably to cover-up their own nonfeasance and malfeasance.*

Corrupt political organizations pervert laws to vilify and falsely prosecute those that oppose their wrongdoing. In reality, the USA is no longer a true democracy; it is controlled by the rich and greedy that prey the naivety of the voters; and, the "masked" tyrants that the rich and greedy put in power.

Most, if not all the laws that I have listed below, were broken by a well-orchestrated crime group that call themselves *"animal rights activists"*. The Attorney General of PA, Kathleen Kane; the DA's in Lebanon, York, and Adams Counties; the FBI; the US Attorney General, Eric Holder; and, the PA Highway Patrol – all ignored my criminal complaints – time-after-time!

Basic human rights are often voided by "free speech" and perverted political and religious views. Ecoterrorism is just a specialized form of terrorism used by *"hooded"* animal activists to exploit those who make their living participating in animal related activities.

After dealing with ecoterrorists for the last fifteen years, I clearly see that their primary motive is personal gain; and, has nothing to do with the love of animals!

I have spent most of my life – starting at the age of 5 – concerned with the animal growth, health, safety, and welfare. With my extensive education and over 60 years of continual experience with animals, I know the difference between legitimate love of animals and ecoterrorism. Mankind has had a special relationship with animals of all kinds since the beginning. I believe that all living creatures have souls; and, it is clear that the human spirit by far is the most corrupt!

> [*The human spirit has been God's biggest concern since the Biblical Creation of Mankind.]

The laws on "ecoterrorism" in Pennsylvania could and should be a redeeming factor for that Commonwealth; however, after spending over three years in that state being terrorized by a perverted non-profit organization, I may be speaking prematurely.

I went to PA mainly because of their lucrative Thoroughbred breeding and racing programs. However, because of their corrupt Justice System, I was egregiously prevented from doing that by a twisted and corrupt organization masquerading as animal rights activists and their undercover ecoterrorists at Penn National Race Track.

It seems that Law Enforcement and the Justice System in PA are selectively ignorant when it comes to ecoterrorism. Or maybe they just choose to ignore the laws concerning ecoterrorism; because, the claims of the crime group's alpha leader are true; she has "people" working for the State Police and the FBI. This is the only reason that I can come up with to answer the question - why does law enforcement ignore obvious evidence and statements arrogantly published stating exactly what the ecoterrorists have as their unlawful objectives - and not prosecute?

Socrates hit the nail squarely on the head when he stated that the reason a man is unjust is because of *ignorance*. It is not the ecoterrorists who are ignorant; they know exactly what they are doing; it is the PA Justice System and the naïve voters who elected its leaders.

As time goes on and the egregious crime of ecoterrorism is continuously ignored, it becomes clear that the real problem lies with undercover members of the corrupt organization that have infiltrated law enforcement. Especially since, the alpha leader of the corrupt organization arrogantly and proudly announces to the world that "her people" have infiltrated and have considerable influence over the State Police and the FBI in PA – the two law enforcement agencies that commonly have the duty and obligation to investigate wrongdoing associated with pari-mutuel horse racing.

Since much of my experience dealing with psychopathic terrorists has been in PA; and, since many of the movies based on true life stories that feature psychopaths seemed to have occurred in Pennsylvania, I will use PA Codes for Crimes and Other Offenses to support my case.

The law entitled "Ecoterrorism" was enacted to protect two very basic human rights: the *"right to work"* in ones chosen line of work; and, the *"right to property"* – the right to own, use, enjoy, and benefit from one's personal property.

Universally, no one has the right to interfere with another's rights to legally work and own property. By doing so, they should forfeit their rights; including, their perverted *right to free speech*; especially, if they are using that right *to pervert the truth and to harm others*.

PA Codes Title 18 Crimes and Offenses: This collective set of laws includes Pennsylvania's crimes and offenses. Laws are supposed to be written so that a fifth grader can understand them.

Then why are the group's obvious criminal activities often ignored by those who could and should do something about them?

> *Why does the Office of the Attorney General of the Commonwealth of Pennsylvania deny that it has the "oversight" to investigate and prosecute corrupt organizations in the state?*

The answer is simple; it has to be willful ignorance of the ecoterrorism laws for personal gain! The laws against ecoterrorism and the well-published terroristic intent of the corrupt organization could not be more transparent.

"A person is guilty of *ecoterrorism* if the person commits a specified offense against property by: intimidating or coercing a person lawfully participating in an activity involving animals, plants, or natural resources;

or preventing or obstructing a person lawfully participating in an activity involving animals, plants, or natural resources." How hard is this law to comprehend?

Furthermore, by its malicious nature, ecoterrorism involves a multitude of other "aggravated" violations of rights, torts, and crimes.

The penalties for some of the crimes and offenses used by ecoterrorists to exploit their victims are: fines up to $250,000 or as much as double the pecuniary gain; up to 40 years imprisonment; and/or, treble the actual damages done to the victim.

In the case of our Charitable Trust and me, treble the actual damages are estimated to be $120 million - in addition to the $40 million in actual damages.

The stiff mandated penalties should tell any sane person, that ecoterrorism is a serious crime; ecoterrorism is a serious felony - not a "civil feud"!!!! It's the same as telling someone who has been repeatedly beaten and robbed by members of a gang that it is a "civil" matter between him and the gang. Ecoterrorism does not carry such harsh criminal penalties because it is a civil matter!

Criminal fines have a dual purpose: to cause the criminals enough economic duress that it will inhibit repeated commission of the crimes and to repay the legal prosecutors for investigating and prosecuting the case. The lack of government funding cannot be a valid excuse in this case, because the payment of the fines and restitution are mandatory. Furthermore, the crimes against my former employer and all its other business relations probably caused over $3 billion in total damages to the local economy!

Terrorists show a pathological disregard for the laws and for the rights of others! These corrupt organizations simply exploit the law and their political views for personal gain!

Violations of Rights, Torts and Crimes

Psychopathic domestic terrorists play by no rules! It is as if they leave no rule or law unbroken. It is as if they stay up at night looking for ways to infringe on the rights of their targeted victims.

Since ecoterrorism is usually *compounded* by corrupt and/or apathetic government officials, their stand-by excuse is that it would cost too much to prosecute the case; or, that it is a civil matter - *no crime has been committed!*

Again the answer to why the crime of ecoterrorism is ignored by law enforcement is simple. Ecoterrorism is politically charged and usually involves corrupt government officials and special interest groups with deep pockets.

As a political out, it appears that law enforcement and the Justice System may take the attitude that all the *false and outrageous allegations against the victim "trump" the deceptive and coercive activities of the ecoterrorists;* however, it is more likely that they make it a civil dispute to cover-up government nonfeasance and malfeasance.

From my experience, the following are some of the many ways domestic terrorists harm their targeted victims:

Violations of Human Rights with Malicious Criminal Intent

1. Right to work
2. Right to property; right to the equal protection of that private property; the right to just compensation for property; and, the right to the use and enjoyment of private property.
3. Right to health and well-being
4. Right to due process and to equal protection
5. Right to privacy and to dignity

Tortuous Acts Committed with Malicious Criminal Intent

6. Defamation, libel, slander, and trade libel
7. False light
8. Tortuous Interference
9. Intentional Infliction of Emotional Distress
10. Negligence Infliction of Emotional Distress

PA Codes Title 18 Crimes and Offenses Committed

11. **§ 309. Duress**
12. **§ 901. Criminal Attempt**
13. **§ 902. Criminal Solicitation**
14. **§ 903. Criminal Conspiracy**
15. **§ 911. Corrupt organizations** - Racketeering
16. **§ 2709.1 Stalking**

17. § 2709. Harassment
18. § 3309. Agricultural vandalism
19. § 3311. Ecoterrorism
20. § 3921. Theft by unlawful taking or disposition
21. § 3922. Theft by deception
22. § 3923. Theft by extortion
23. § 3925. Receiving stolen property
24. § 4701. Bribery in official and political matters
25. § 4702. Threats and other improper influence in official and political matters
26. § 4906. False reports to law enforcement authorities; (a) falsely incriminate another and (b) Fictitious reports
27. § 4910. Tampering with or fabricating physical evidence;
28. § 5107. Aiding consummation of crime
29. § 5108. Compounding
30. § 5111. Dealing in proceeds of unlawful activities
31. § 5301. Official oppression
32. § 5511. Cruelty to animals
33. § 5741. Unlawful access to stored communications
34. § 6301. Corruption of minors
35. § 7102. Administering drugs to race horses
36. § 7611. Unlawful use of computer and other computer crimes
37. § 7612. Disruption of service
38. § 7613. Computer theft
39. § 7614. Unlawful duplication
40. § 7616. Distribution of computer virus.

The State of Tennessee and the Nashville Metropolitan Government maliciously harassed me for a number of years in retaliation for me standing up to a number of corrupt government employees in that state. As a matter of fact, some of the Nashville coconspirators jointed the conspiracy and played a substantial role in the ecoterrorism in PA. The Nashville coconspirators were *insanely obsessed* with preventing me from practicing veterinary medicine in Tennessee – or any other state!!

The ecoterrorists in PA were also *insanely obsessed* with *preventing me from practicing veterinary medicine and from participating in Thoroughbred breeding and racing* – the primary element of committing the crime of ecoterrorism. Stealing most of the Trust's horses by using theft related criminal offenses and then harming and killing many of them - pretty much take care of the other element of ecoterrorism – offenses against property.

Since law enforcement has ignored these despicable crimes, it really looks like the alpha leader of the crime group was right when she arrogantly bragged that some of "her people" work for the State Police and the FBI. It is obvious that some of her people also work for Penn National Gaming and the News Media. Other members of the crime group were working undercover for my former employer, Star Barn Thoroughbreds; while others undercover members were posing as clients, friends, and business relations of SBT and the Trust.

Pennsylvania also has agricultural vandalism laws (misdemeanors or felonies, depending on pecuniary loss), and a law prohibiting the destruction of agricultural crops (felony). Although my former employer Star Barn Thoroughbreds and our Charitable Trust were deprived of their rights and their property, absolutely nothing was done; except, the continual one-sided investigations of all the false and fictitious reports sent in by affiliates of the crime group.

All the false and fictitious reports (from people all over the country who had never seen the horses) were continually and thoroughly investigated (in hope of finding something wrong); but for some reason, continually *filing false reports and killing and stealing horses were not worthy of being investigated* in the eyes of PA law enforcement; those crimes was wrongfully considered to be civil matters by the local, state and federal government agencies that had legal duties and obligations to investigate and prosecute.

I believe that these government agencies refused to investigate my complaints, because they either knew and/or they soon found out that their own agencies had been infiltrated by the ecoterrorists; thus, making them culpable for *compounding* the offenses. Either that or they were too embarrassed for being so easily manipulated and duped by the ecoterrorists.

I was actually *reprimanded* by a couple of these law enforcement officials for filing my complaints and citing the applicable laws!!!!

Back to the Facts of Law:

Pursuant to PA Title 18 Chapter 33 § 3311: *Ecoterrorism* – a person is guilty of ecoterrorism if the person commits a specified offense against *property* intending to do any of the following: (1) *Intimidate or coerce* an individual *lawfully*: (i) *participating in an activity involving animals* ... (2) *Prevent or obstruct* an individual from *lawfully*: (i) *participating in an activity involving animals* ...

Pursuant to PA Title 18 § 3311: Ecoterrorism as used in this section, the following words and phrases shall have the meanings given to them in this subsection: "Activity involving animals or plants."

A lawful activity involving the use of animals, including any of the following: (5) *Entertainment and recreation.* (6) *Research, teaching* ... (8)

Agricultural activity and farming as defined in section 3309 (relating to agricultural vandalism).

Pursuant to PA Title 18 Chapter 33 § 3309: *Agricultural vandalism.* (c) Definition.--As used in this section, the terms "agricultural activity" and "farming" include *public and private research activity, ... the commercial production of* agricultural crops, *livestock* or livestock products...

Pursuant to PA Title 18 Chapter 39 § 3901: Definitions. *"Property" Anything of value, including real estate, tangible and intangible personal property, contract rights, choses-in-action and other interests in or claims to ... domestic animals....*

Pursuant to agriculture vandalism and ecoterrorism statutes, the *specified offenses* against property include *damage to tangible or intangible personal property, contract rights, choices-in-action and other interest in or claim to domestic animals.*

As a matter of law, specified offenses pertaining to ecoterrorism include *unlawful taking and disposition* of livestock used in agriculture activities.

As a matter of law, a person commits the offense of agricultural vandalism if he intentionally or recklessly ... damages the real or tangible personal property of another, where *the property defaced, marked or otherwise damaged is used in agricultural activity or farming.*

I think that stealing and killing horses used for *"Entertainment and recreation"*; **Agriculture activity**; and, *"Research, teaching ..."* is also pretty damaging – and damning!

As a matter of law, horse racing and breeding are agricultural activities, which are regulated by the PA Department of Agriculture. As a matter of law, being maliciously deprived of entering the backstretch of the *Penn National Gaming deprived me of property - in the form of a vital choice in action.* It also violated *my rights; the free enterprise laws; and, our right to fairly compete* at those tracks.

The Penn National Gaming policy on selling horses to a slaughter house is in itself contrary to the "ecoterrorism" statute; since, selling a horse to slaughter is a legal right of the owner and a common agricultural practice. *Selling any animal that you own, privately or at a public auction, is morally and legally accepted.*

This policy is a way for the undercover members of the crime group to falsely vilify and to obstruct and/or prevent one of their targets from participating in Thoroughbred racing at any of the Penn National Gaming para-mutual tracks; especially in my case, because *the outrageous lies that I sent horses to slaughter and starved and abused horses were impossible and insane; I had no horses under my care, custody, or control at the times these false allegations were brought against me.*

Ecoterrorists often mislabel public auctions as "killer" or "slaughter" sales; this is just an integral part of their crime scheme; a way of misleading and outraging the public and fraudulently soliciting donations by creating "shock" value.

Those who know me, know that I am deeply disturbed by the thought of killing a healthy animal of any kind; and, that sending a horse to a slaughter house is not something that I would do.

Theft related offenses as described in PA Codes Title 18 Chapter 39 are specified offences commonly used to commit Ecoterrorism.

PA Title 18 Chapter 39 § 3901: Definitions. *"Deprive."* (1) To *withhold property of another permanently* or for so extended a period as to appropriate a major portion of its economic value, or with intent to restore only upon payment of reward or other compensation; or (2) *to dispose of the property so as to make it unlikely that the owner will recover it.*

PA Title 18 Chapter 39 § 3901: Definitions. *"Property of another"* - Includes property in which *any person other than the actor* has an interest which *the actor is not privileged to infringe,* regardless of the fact that the actor also has an interest in the property and regardless of the fact that the other person might be precluded from civil recovery because the property was used in an unlawful transaction or was subject to forfeiture as contraband.

PA Title 18 Chapter 39 § 3921: *Theft by unlawful taking or disposition.* (a) Movable property.--A person is guilty of theft if he unlawfully takes, or exercises unlawful control over, movable property of another with intent to deprive him thereof.

PA Title 18 Chapter 39 § 3922: *Theft by deception.* (a) Offense defined.--A person is guilty of theft if he intentionally obtains or withholds property of another by deception. A person deceives if he intentionally:

(1) *creates or reinforces a false impression,* including false impressions as to law, value, intention or other state of mind; (2) *prevents another from acquiring information which would affect his judgment of a transaction*; or, (3) *fails to correct a false impression which the deceiver previously created or reinforced, or which the deceiver knows to be influencing another* to whom he stands in a fiduciary or confidential relationship.

PA Title 18 Chapter 39 § 3923: *Theft by extortion.* (a) Offense defined.--A person is guilty of theft if he intentionally obtains or withholds property of another by threatening to: (1) **commit another criminal offense**; (2) *accuse anyone of a criminal offense*; (3) expose any secret tending to *subject any person to hatred, contempt or ridicule*; (4) *take or withhold action as an official,* or *cause an official to take or withhold action*; (5) bring about or continue a strike, *boycott* or other *collective unofficial* *action, if the property is not demanded or received for the benefit of the group in whose interest the actor purports to act;* (6) *testify or provide information or withhold testimony or information with respect to the legal claim or defense of another;* or (7) *inflict any other harm which would not benefit the actor.*

PA Title 18 Chapter 39 § 3925: *Receiving stolen property.* (a) Offense defined.--A person is guilty of theft if he *intentionally receives, retains, or disposes of movable property of another knowing that it has been stolen, or believing that it has probably been stolen,* unless the property is received, retained, or disposed with intent to restore it to the owner.

(b) Definition.--As used in this section the word *"receiving" means acquiring possession, control or title,* or lending on the security of the property.

The following are other offenses used by ecoterrorists to intimidate and coerce their targeted owners with the intent to prevent and obstruct them from participating in Thoroughbred racing and breeding:

PA Title 18 Chapter 9 § 901: *Criminal attempt;* (a) Definition of attempt.--A person commits an attempt when, with intent to commit a specific crime, he does any act which constitutes a substantial step toward the commission of that crime.

(c) Renunciation. -- (1) In any prosecution for an attempt to commit a crime, it is a defense that, under circumstances manifesting a voluntary and complete renunciation of his criminal intent, the defendant avoided the commission of the crime attempted by abandoning his criminal effort and, if the mere abandonment was insufficient to accomplish such avoidance, by taking further and affirmative steps which prevented the commission thereof.

(2) A renunciation is not "voluntary and complete" within the meaning of this subsection if it is motivated in whole or part by: (i) a belief that circumstances exist which increase the probability of detection or apprehension of the defendant or another participant in the criminal enterprise, or which render more difficult the accomplishment of the criminal purpose; or (ii) a decision to postpone the criminal conduct until another time or to transfer the criminal effort to another victim or another but similar objective.

> *[*Ecoterrorism is nothing but terrorism veiled as a perverted political cause.]*

PA Title 18 Chapter 9 § 902: *Criminal solicitation;* (a) Definition of solicitation.--A person is guilty of solicitation to commit a crime if with the intent of promoting or facilitating its commission he commands, encourages or requests another person to engage in specific conduct which would constitute such crime or an attempt to commit such crime or which would establish his complicity in its commission or attempted commission.

(b) Renunciation.--It is a defense that the actor, after soliciting another person to commit a crime, persuaded him not to do so or otherwise prevented the commission of the crime, under circumstances manifesting a complete and voluntary renunciation of his criminal intent.

Title 18 Chapter 9 § 903: *Criminal conspiracy*; (a) Definition of conspiracy.--A person is guilty of conspiracy with another person or persons to commit a crime if with *the intent of promoting or facilitating* its commission he:

(1) Agrees with such other person or persons that they or one or more of them will engage in conduct which constitutes such crime or an attempt or solicitation to commit such crime; or

(2) Agrees to aid such other person or persons in the planning or commission of such crime or of an attempt or solicitation to commit such crime.

(b) Scope of conspiratorial relationship.--If a person guilty of conspiracy, as defined by subsection (a) of this section, *knows that a person with whom he conspires to commit a crime has conspired with another person or persons to commit the same crime,* he is guilty of conspiring with such other person or persons, to commit such crime **whether or not he knows their identity**.

(c) *Conspiracy with multiple criminal objectives*.-If a person conspires to commit a number of crimes; he is guilty of only one conspiracy so long as such multiple crimes are the object of the same agreement or continuous conspiratorial relationship.

(i) no defendant shall be charged with a conspiracy in any county other than one in which he entered into such conspiracy or in which an overt act pursuant to such conspiracy was done by him or by a person with whom he conspired;

(e) *Overt act*.--No person may be convicted of conspiracy to commit a crime unless an overt act in pursuance of such conspiracy is alleged and proved to have been done by him or by a person with whom he conspired.

(f) Renunciation.--It is a defense that the actor, after conspiring to commit a crime, thwarted the success of the conspiracy, under circumstances manifesting a complete and voluntary renunciation of his criminal intent.

(g) *Duration of conspiracy*.--For purposes of 42 Pa.C.S. § 5552

---

(1) *Conspiracy is a continuing course of conduct which terminates when the crime or crimes which are its object are committed or the agreement that they be committed is abandoned by the defendant and by those with whom he conspired;*

(2) *Such abandonment is presumed if neither the defendant nor anyone with whom he conspired does any overt act in pursuance of the conspiracy during the applicable period of limitation; and*

(3) If an individual abandons the agreement, the conspiracy is terminated as to him only if and when he advises those with whom he conspired of his abandonment or he informs the law enforcement authorities of the existence of the conspiracy and of his participation therein.

PA Title 18 Chapter 9 § 911: *Corrupt organizations*; (a) Findings of fact.--The General Assembly finds that:

(1) organized crime is a highly sophisticated, diversified, and widespread phenomenon which *annually drains billions of dollars from the national economy* by various *patterns of unlawful conduct* including the illegal use of force, fraud, and corruption;

(2) *Organized crime exists on a large scale within the Commonwealth of Pennsylvania*, engaging in the same patterns of unlawful conduct which characterize its activities nationally;

(3) the vast amounts of money and power accumulated by organized crime are increasingly *used to infiltrate and corrupt legitimate businesses* operating within the Commonwealth, together with *all of the techniques of violence, intimidation, and other forms of unlawful conduct through which such money and power are derived;*

(4) in furtherance of such infiltration and corruption, *organized crime utilizes and applies to its unlawful purposes laws of the Commonwealth of Pennsylvania* conferring and relating to the privilege of engaging in various types of business and designed to insure that such businesses are conducted in furtherance of the public interest and the general economic welfare of the Commonwealth;

(5) such infiltration and corruption provide an outlet for illegally obtained capital, harm innocent investors, entrepreneurs, merchants and consumers, *interfere with free competition,* and thereby *constitute a substantial danger to the economic and general welfare of the Commonwealth of Pennsylvania*; and

(6) in order to successfully resist and eliminate this situation, it is necessary to provide *new remedies and procedures.*

(b) Prohibited activities. –

---

(2) It shall be unlawful for any person through a pattern of racketeering activity to ... *control of any enterprise.*

(3) It shall be unlawful for any person employed by or associated with any enterprise *to conduct or participate, directly or indirectly, in the conduct of such enterprise's affairs through a **pattern of racketeering activity***.

(4) It shall be unlawful for any person to conspire to violate any of the provisions of paragraphs (1), (2) or (3) of this subsection.

(c) Grading.--Whoever violates any provision of subsection (b) of this section is guilty of *a felony of the first degree*. A violation of this subsection shall be deemed to continue so long as the person who committed the violation continues to receive any benefit from the violation.

(d) Civil remedies.—

(1) The several courts of common pleas, and the Commonwealth Court, shall have jurisdiction to *prevent and restrain violations of subsection* (b) of this section by issuing appropriate orders, including but not limited to: (i) *ordering any person to divest himself of any interest direct or indirect, in the* enterprise; *imposing reasonable restrictions on the future activities or investments of any person*, including but not limited to, *prohibiting any person from engaging in the same type of endeavor as the enterprise engaged in*; and (ii) making due provision for the rights of innocent persons, *ordering the dissolution of the enterprise, ordering the denial, suspension or revocation of charters of domestic corporations*, certificates of authority authorizing foreign corporations to do business within the Commonwealth of Pennsylvania, licenses, permits, or prior approval granted to any enterprise by any department or agency of the Commonwealth of Pennsylvania; or *prohibiting the enterprise from engaging in any business*.

(2) In any proceeding under this subsection, the court shall proceed as soon as practicable to the hearing and determination thereof. Pending final determination, the court may enter preliminary or *special injunctions*, or take such other actions, including the acceptance of satisfactory performance bonds, as it may deem proper.

(3) *A final judgment or decree rendered in favor of the Commonwealth of Pennsylvania in any criminal proceeding under this section shall estop the defendant from denying the essential allegations of the criminal offense in any subsequent civil proceeding under this subsection.*

(4) Proceedings under this subsection, at pretrial, trial and appellate levels, shall be governed by the Pennsylvania Rules of Civil Procedure and all other rules and procedures relating to civil actions, except to the extent inconsistent with the provisions of this section.

(e) *Enforcement.* –

(1) The *Attorney General shall have the **power and duty to enforce** the provisions of this section*, including the authority to issue civil investigative demands pursuant to subsection (f), institute proceedings under subsection (d), and to take such actions as may be necessary to ascertain and investigate alleged violations of this section.

(2) The *Attorney General* and the *district attorneys of the several counties shall have concurrent authority to institute criminal proceedings under the provisions of this section.*

(3) *Nothing contained in this subsection shall be construed to limit the regulatory or investigative authority of any department or agency of the Commonwealth* whose functions might relate to persons, enterprises, or matters falling within the scope of this section.

(h) Definitions.--As used in this section: (1) *"Racketeering activity"* means all of the following: (i) an act which is indictable under any of the following provisions of this title: Section 2706 (relating to *terroristic threats*)

Title 18 Chapter 27 § 2709: *Harassment*; (a) Offense defined.--A person commits the **crime of harassment** when, with *intent to harass, annoy or alarm another*, the person:

(1) strikes, shoves, kicks or otherwise subjects the other person to physical contact, or attempts or *threatens to do the same*;

(2) follows the other person in or about a public place or places;

(3) *engages in a course of conduct or repeatedly commits acts* **which serve no legitimate purpose**;

(4) *communicates to or about such other person any lewd, lascivious, threatening or obscene words, language,* **drawings or caricatures**;

(5) *communicates repeatedly in an anonymous manner*;

(6) *communicates repeatedly at extremely inconvenient hours*;

Title 18 Chapter 27 § 2709.1: **Stalking**; (a) Offense defined.--A person commits the **crime of stalking** when the person either;

(1) engages *in a course of conduct or repeatedly commits acts* toward another person, including *following the person without proper authority,* **under circumstances which demonstrate either an intent to**

place such other person in reasonable fear of bodily injury or *to cause substantial emotional distress* to such other person;

(2) *Engages in a course of conduct or repeatedly communicates to another person under circumstances which demonstrate or communicate either intent to place such other person in reasonable fear of bodily injury or to cause substantial emotional distress to such other person.*

(b) Venue. –

(1) An offense committed under this section may be deemed to have been committed at either the place at which the communication or communications were made or at the place where the communication or communications were received.

(2) Acts indicating a course of conduct which occur in more than one jurisdiction may be used by any other jurisdiction in which an act occurred as *evidence of a continuing pattern of conduct or a course of conduct.*

Title 18 Chapter 47 § 4701: *Bribery in official and political matters*; (a) Offenses defined.--A person is guilty of bribery, a *felony of the third degree*, if he offers, confers or agrees to confer upon another, or solicits, accepts or agrees to accept from another:

(1) *any pecuniary benefit* as consideration for the decision, opinion, recommendation, vote or other exercise of discretion as a *public servant*, party official or voter by the recipient;

(2) any benefit as consideration for the decision, vote, recommendation or other exercise of official discretion by the recipient in a judicial, administrative or legislative proceeding; or

(3) Any benefit as consideration for *a violation of a known legal duty as public servant or party official.*

PA Title 18 Chapter 47 § 4702: *Threats and other improper influence in official and political matters*; (a) Offenses defined.--A person commits an offense if he:

(1) threatens unlawful harm to any person with intent to influence his decision, opinion, recommendation, vote or other exercise of discretion as a public servant, party official or voter;

(2) *threatens unlawful harm to any public servant with intent to influence his decision, opinion, recommendation, vote or other exercise of discretion in a judicial or administrative proceeding*; or

(3) *threatens unlawful harm to any public servant or party official with intent to influence him to violate his known legal duty.*

PA Title 18 Chapter 49 § 4906: *False reports to law enforcement authorities*;

(a) **Falsely incriminating another.**--Except as provided in subsection (c), *a person who knowingly gives false information to any law enforcement officer with intent to implicate another* commits a *misdemeanor of the second degree.*

(b) *Fictitious reports.*--Except as provided in subsection (c), a person commits a *misdemeanor of the third degree* if he:

(1) *reports to law enforcement authorities an offense or other incident within their concern knowing that it did not occur*; or

(2) *pretends to furnish such authorities with information relating to an offense or incident when he knows he has no information relating to such offense or incident.*

PA Title 18 Chapter 49 § 4910: *Tampering with or fabricating physical evidence*; A person commits a misdemeanor of the second degree if, believing that an official proceeding or investigation is pending or about to be instituted, he:

(1) *alters, destroys, conceals, or removes any record, document or thing with intent to impair its verity or availability in such proceeding or investigation*; or

(2) *makes, presents, or uses any record, document or thing knowing it to be false and with intent to mislead a public servant who is or may be engaged in such proceeding or investigation.*

PA Title 18 Chapter 51 **§ 5107:** *Aiding consummation of crime*;

(a) Offense defined.--**A person commits an offense if he intentionally aids another to accomplish an unlawful object of a crime, as by safeguarding the proceeds thereof or** *converting the proceeds into negotiable funds.*

(b) Grading.--*The offense is a **felony of the third degree** if the principal offense was a felony of the first or second degree.* Otherwise it is a misdemeanor of the second degree.

PA Title 18 Chapter 51 § 5108: **Compounding**; (a) Offense defined.--A person commits a *misdemeanor of the second degree* if he accepts or agrees to *accept any pecuniary benefit* in consideration of refraining from reporting to law enforcement authorities the commission or suspected commission of any offense or information relating to an offense.

PA Title 18 Chapter 51 § 5111: **Dealing in proceeds of unlawful activities**; (a) Offense defined.--A person commits *a felony of the first degree* if the person conducts a financial transaction under any of the following circumstances:

(1) With knowledge that the property involved, including *stolen or illegally obtained property*, represents *the proceeds of unlawful*

activity, the person acts with the **intent to promote the carrying on of the unlawful activity.**

(2) With knowledge that the property involved, including **stolen or illegally obtained property,** represents the proceeds of unlawful activity and that **the transaction is designed in whole or in part to conceal or disguise the nature, location, source, ownership or control of the proceeds of unlawful activity.**

(3) To avoid a transaction reporting requirement under State or Federal law.

(b) Penalty.--Upon conviction of a violation under subsection (a), *a person shall be sentenced to* **a fine of the greater of $100,000 or twice the value of the property involved in the transaction or to imprisonment for not more than 20 years, or both.**

(c) Civil penalty.--A person who conducts or attempts to conduct a transaction described in subsection (a) is liable to the Commonwealth for a civil penalty of the greater of:

(1) **The value of the property, funds or monetary instruments involved in the transaction;**

(d) Cumulative remedies.--Any proceedings under this section **shall be in addition to any other criminal penalties or forfeitures authorized under the State law.**

(e) **Enforcement.** –

(1) The **Attorney General** *shall have the* **power and duty** *to institute proceedings to recover the civil penalty provided under subsection* (c) against any person liable to the Commonwealth for such a penalty.

(2) The **district attorneys of the several counties** shall have authority to investigate and to institute criminal proceedings for any violation of subsection (a).

(3) In addition to the authority conferred upon the Attorney General by the act of October 15, 1980 (P.L.950, No.164), known as the Commonwealth Attorneys Act, the **Attorney General** *shall have the authority* **to investigate and to institute criminal proceedings** *for any violation of subsection*

(a) *or any series of related violations involving more than one county of the Commonwealth or involving any county of the Commonwealth and another state. No person charged with a violation of subsection (a) by the Attorney General shall have standing to challenge the authority of the Attorney General to investigate or prosecute the case,* and, if any such challenge is made, the challenge shall be dismissed and no relief shall be available in the courts of the Commonwealth to the person making the challenge.

(4) Nothing contained in this subsection shall be construed to limit the regulatory or investigative authority of any department or agency of the Commonwealth whose functions might relate to persons, enterprises or matters falling within the scope of this section.

PA Title 18 Chapter 53 § 5301: *Official oppression*; A person acting or purporting to act in an official capacity or taking advantage of such actual or purported capacity commits a misdemeanor of the second degree if, knowing that his conduct is illegal, he:

(1) *subjects another to arrest, detention, search, seizure, mistreatment, dispossession, assessment, lien or other infringement of personal or property rights; or*

(2) *denies or impedes another in the exercise or enjoyment of any right, privilege, power or immunity.*

PA Title 18 Chapter § 5741: *Unlawful access to stored communications.* (b) Penalty. -- (1) if the offense is committed for *the purpose of commercial advantage, malicious destruction or damage, or private commercial gain*, the offender shall be subject to: (i) *a fine of not more than $250,000 or imprisonment for not more than one year, or both*, in the case of a first offense; or

PA Title 18 Chapter 63 **§ 6301**: *Corruption of minors*; (a) Offense defined. -- (1) (i) Except as provided in subparagraph (ii), whoever, being of the age of 18 years and upwards, by any act *corrupts or tends to corrupt the morals of any minor less than 18 years of age, or who aids, abets, entices or encourages any such minor in the commission of any crime*... commits a misdemeanor of the first degree.

PA Title 18 Chapter 71 § 7102: *Administering drugs to race horses*; A person is guilty of a misdemeanor of the first degree if he administers drugs or stimulants with the *intent to affect the speed of horses in races where there is a monetary award offered.*

PA Title 18 Chapter 76 **§ 7611**: *Unlawful use of computer and other computer crimes.*

PA Title 18 Chapter 76 **§ 7612**: *Disruption of service*; (a) Offense defined.--A person commits an offense if he *intentionally or knowingly engages in a scheme* or artifice, including, but not limited to, a denial of service attack upon any computer, computer system, computer network, computer software, computer program, computer server, computer database, *World Wide Web site* or telecommunication device or any part thereof that is *designed to block, impede or deny the access of information or initiation or* *completion of any sale or transaction by users of that computer*, computer system, computer network, computer software, computer program, computer server or database or any part thereof. (b) Grading.--An offense under this section shall constitute a *felony of the third degree.*

PA Title 18 Chapter 76 **§ 7613: *Computer theft***; (a) **Offense** defined.--A person commits an offense if he *unlawfully accesses or exceeds his authorization to access any data from a computer*, computer system or computer network or takes or copies any supporting documentation whether existing or residing internal or external to a computer, computer system or computer network of another with the intent to deprive him thereof.

(b) Grading.--An offense under this section shall constitute a felony of the third degree.

PA Title 18 Chapter 76 **§ 7614: *Unlawful duplication***

PA Title 18 Chapter 76 **§ 7616: *Distribution of computer virus*.**

On several occasions my computers were hacked. On at least three occasions, my computers were hacked and most of my business data, records, and documents were downloaded and/or deleted and the computers were crashed and had to be replaced. On several other occasions my e-mall account was hacked and all my business and personal contacts were delete; then, my contacts were sent a number of scams allegedly from me - using my email address.

Because of computer related crimes, I have been forced to take my business computer off-line.

[*I hate to ridicule and be sarcastic; because, that is how ecoterrorists are. However, the following is my *satirical* depiction the fallacies and ignorance of ecoterrorists; their insane crime schemes; and, how it is compounded by corrupt law enforcement:

The deceptive and coercive practices of ecoterrorist are almost as despicable and unreasonable as telling a gang rape victim that - "the rapists *accused* you of being a whore; therefore, it is a civil matter between you and the rapists, because *they were just using their freedom of expression*. And by the way - *you are under investigation* for prostitution.

One more thing - this crazy lady for California and 'her people' from all over the country are working undercover with the rapists. They said that you sell your kids to cannibals - and that you beat and starve your kids.

And because this psychopath and her 'following' also work undercover with social services and law enforcement, they are justified and privileged to come to your house and seize your kids. You know - to rescue them from cannibalism, abuse and starvation.

And one last thing - if you try to get your kids back, we will kill all of them and put you *and your spouse* in jail for prostitution and for selling your kids. Then we will take your house and *urgently* sell it so we have the money that it *would have* cost us to care for your *mediocre and deformed* kids while we *pretend* to find them good homes; even though, some of them have already died and the rest have been sold into slavery to cover our expenses for 'rescuing' them."]

CHAPTER 7

Psychological Profile of Terrorists

The characteristics of domestic and foreign terrorists are basically the same as those of psychopaths. Simply put - terrorists are psychopaths. They play by their own rules; in their twisted minds, their victims have no rights. Terroristic in-groups use the same methods and techniques that are used by psychopaths to dupe and manipulate their victims, accomplices, and benefactors. It's like they write books on *How to Be a Terrorist While Appearing to be Fighting a Noble Political, Charitable, or Religious Cause*.

Terrorism takes on many forms – depending on the "noble cause". I will primarily cover anti-Thoroughbred Racing ecoterrorism. After experiencing and scrutinizing their mode of operation and signature crime schemes, the primary reason anti-Thoroughbred Racing terrorists chose to exploit the Thoroughbred industry is because *that is where the money and valuable property is*!! Terrorists don't specialize in exploiting the poor; however, the poor and innocent are often consequential victims. Furthermore, terrorists are usually well-organized and operate as a pack or in-group. As a matter of law, terrorists usually operate as *well-organized crime groups*.

"The first clue is "duping". – R. Hare. Terrorists trick, con, and dupe people into believing strange or outrageous lies; they often make up stories just to see if they *can* get away with them. If they do, it feeds their narcissistic belief that others are stupid and that they are superior. Their mode of operation is based on a fallacy used to prey on ignorance - *argumentum ad ignorantiam*. Or they may fallaciously appeal to a higher power – even though they are not intrinsically inspired by a Holy Spirit!!

Terrorists often need "duped" accomplices to carry-out their elaborate crime schemes. Therefore, they often infiltrate legitimate charitable organizations, religious groups, and government agencies. And of course, infiltrating the News Media helps facilitate their crimes by publically reinforcing false impressions.

The duped "following" does the dirty work and parrots the outrageous lies, while the psychopathic leaders rake in the donations for their perverted terroristic organizations.

[*Note: Socrates rationalized that unjust men do evil out of ignorance; and, only when men are wise will they choose to do what is just. He also argued that the "evil" in a thing will eventually destroy it – like rust will destroy iron and government corruption will destroy any state. Socrates also rationalized that the evil in a man's soul does not destroy it; therefore, our souls must be immortal. This is where a higher power comes in; therefore, the greater of a citizen's rewards and punishments will come to their souls in a life after death – in Heaven or Hades.]

A favored psychopathic technique of domestic terrorists is to publically vilify their targets by fabricating vicious lies and continually parroting them on the Internet; then they reinforce the despicable lies by sarcastically questionings the vilified victim's honesty, integrity, trustworthiness, motives, character, competence, skills, sanity and judgment!

By using an owner's employees to covertly sabotage their agriculture operation and to frame the owner, ecoterrorists covertly weaken the victim until they feels that they can totally control the victim; at which time, they goes for a well-published takeover of the victimized owner's assets. In the case of anti-Thoroughbred Racing ecoterrorists, they demand that the owner turn their valuable Thoroughbreds over to "their people". If the owner refused, then the ecoterrorists lets the owner know that they will not stop at *anything* until that happens and/or the owner is out of the Thoroughbred business.

Even after I was on to the ecoterrorists, I was still faced with the real threat of the ecoterrorists harming or killing our horses. Now I know, even if the ecoterrorists gained control of the horses, most of them were still doomed to death! Their value to the terrorists was to create "shock value" which the terrorists use to raise donations.

Like kidnappers - ecoterrorists are not concerned with the health, safety, and welfare of victims or their animals; they are more interested in the *ransom* – in this case fraudulently solicited and/or coerced donations to their perverted tax-exempt organizations. Once the ecoterrorists take possession of the animals, they are *expendable.* A dead kidnapping victim cannot talk; and, as the anti-Thoroughbred Racing ecoterrorists like to say, *"You couldn't run a dead horse".* Ironically, (to terrorists) their victims are more valuable dead than alive!

There are many duped accomplices and benefactors who aid and abet terroristic in-groups without realizing that they have been subtly and masterfully manipulated. In my case, several accomplices were easily duped by the alpha leader and her juvenile saboteur who was working undercover for my former employer. It is now clear that the alpha leader and her young apprentice committed these crimes for personal gain. The alpha leader fraudulently solicited donations and the apprentice got her share of the spoils – three high-quality Thoroughbred horses – and they both wanted more!!!!

The alpha leader and "her people" have an insane sense of entitlement to anything that may be of values to their victims. They get a perverted sense of pleasure from taking away things that was near-and-dear to their victims (happiness, health, career, dreams, esteem, good reputation, employment, and beloved Thoroughbred horses) - anything that may be valued by the victim - or *coveted* by a member of their crime group.

One of the signature scams of the anti-Thoroughbred Racing terrorists is the malicious mislabeling of targeted public horse auctions as "killer sales" or "slaughter sales"; even though these sales are public auctions and their primary purpose is to market companion or pleasure horses. Any identifiable Thoroughbred that is consigned to one of these public auctions is deceptively mislabeled as "sent to slaughter" or "sent to a kill pen".

Animals misrepresented as being *sent to slaughter* and animals misrepresented as being *starved and abused* create public outrageous intended to vilify the owners and the "shock value" needed to raise donations – even though it is all fabricated!

According to leading psychologists Robert D. Hare and Paul Babiak, psychopaths are always on the lookout for individuals to scam or swindle. Anti-Thoroughbred Racing terrorists specialized in exploiting Thoroughbred owners, top management, trainers and breeders; the heart of the industry. Vulnerable owners and trainers are like geese that lay golden eggs. This is why I don't believe these people really want to see the demise of the whole flock (the Thoroughbred industry). These people make their despicable living off their fabricated dark side of Thoroughbred Racing. They target the people who represent the bright side of Thoroughbred Racing; or it my case, because I also recognized their camouflaged crime scheme and posed a threat to their well-organized crime organization.

Non-targeted participants in the Thoroughbred industry take the apathetic approach; they simply ignore the terroristic activities; because, "it's not our problem".

Anti-Thoroughbred Racing terrorists specifically exploit the Thoroughbred industry by: targeting Thoroughbred owners, breeders and trainers; deceiving, manipulating, and/or coercing law enforcement, especially local Humane Societies, the State Police, and the FBI; coercing race tracks and filmmakers; exploiting public horse auctions; conning the legitimate animal lovers into making donations; and, duping accomplices into aiding and abetting their criminal activities for secret rewards.

Altruistic, honest, naïve, and trusting people are easy targets for psychopathic in-groups, because truly good people sometimes find it hard to believe that other human beings can be so evil, devious, and ruthless; especially, since the undercover ecoterrorists are sometimes trusted employees, friends, business associates, track officials, government officials, and even clients.

Because the Thoroughbred industry is so competitive, *vilifying* the targeted victims is probably the most powerful manipulation tactic. It puts the victims on the defensive; while masking the criminal intent of the ecoterrorists. Others in the industry are often duped into believing the lies; or, they may ostracize the victims to placate the ecoterrorists - fearing that if they don't support the terrorists, they may become the next target.

Some co-dependent accomplices are even duped into aiding and abetting the crimes just to gain social favor with the ecoterrorists.

True to their psychopathic nature, ecoterrorists will not stop until their target has been completely destroyed - financially, socially, professionally, and emotionally; and, members of the crime group have deprived the owner of the horses by theft and/or by death.

Ecoterrorists leave owners without necessities: horses; loyal employees; clients; a place to market their horses; or, a place to race their horses. The targeted owners and trainers are maliciously prevented from participating in Thoroughbred Racing. All they can do is shake their heads and ask - *why would anyone want to compete in such a corrupt and hostile environment?*

The manipulative techniques used most by terroristic crime groups are: lying, lying by omission, denial, covert intimidation, guilt tripping, shaming, vilifying the victim, self-serving agendas cloaked as noble causes, superficial charm, flattery, blaming others, and the *betrayal of trust and confidence.*

Ecoterrorists will even degrade the innocent horses; that is until they have gained control of them. Once the horses are in their control (or dead), the psychopaths will then *gloat* on how noble and great the horses are.

I was a model Thoroughbred trainer and owner. I played by the rules. I rarely run my horses on medication and I discouraged exercise riders and jockeys from using whips on my horses. It did not bother me that all the other horses in the race was on Bute and Lasix; I never saw the benefits. I had horses that ran close to track record times and won numerous stakes races without running on medication.

In the past, I had as many as 80 horses in training at a time, yet I never had a horse-in-training loss their lives due to injury or other illness. I treated my horses like friends and family - with love and respect. And I adamantly would not let my staff disrespect a horse. *Whether you are talking to a person, or an animal, praise is the best motivator! Horses also have a sixth sense and can tell what you think of them!*

My impeccable record as a veterinarian, trainer, farm manager, and bloodstock agent is probably why I became a victim of those that like to cast a dark shadow on Thoroughbred Racing. As for the trainers and owners who did not play by the rules, they just provide the ecoterrorists with fuel to propel their sinister crime schemes.

[*I want the reader to learn some important lessons; therefore, I will repeat things that the reader needs to know and understand about psychopaths, terrorists, tyrants, and corrupt government officials! However, it has been my observation that people do not learn from the mistakes or bad experiences of others as well as they should; often thinking this will not happen to me. People learn more from their own mistakes and bad experiences.]

CHAPTER 8

Common Targets of Anti-Racing Terrorists

Anti-Thoroughbred Racing terrorists have infiltrated and have considerable influence and control over: the Thoroughbred Industry, especially in the Mid-Atlantic states; law enforcement agencies, including local humane societies, animal control, State Police, and the FBI; other non-profit organizations, including the ASPCA, HSUS, and PETA; open public horse auctions; the News Media; and, Thoroughbred race tracks.

The following are the potential targets & victims of anti-Thoroughbred Racing terrorists; they specialize in exploiting the Thoroughbred Industry and anyone that participates in Thoroughbred Racing:

Thoroughbred Owners - including their management, employees, trainers, veterinarians, clients, and other business relations - and, their *high-quality* Thoroughbred horses; Targeted Public Horse Auctions; Film Producers (Thoroughbred related shows or movies; such as "Luck"); Thoroughbred Race Tracks & Officials; Former Thoroughbred Owners and Breeders (to shame or coerce them into making donations); Law Enforcement & Justice System; News Media; General Public; Accomplices (people that do the dirty work and can be blamed if things go wrong); Thoroughbred Industry (anti-racing agenda); Consequential Victims; and, Members of their in-groups that do not play their conspiratorial roles to the satisfaction of the Crime Group.

CHAPTER 9

Signature Crime Scheme

*[*Note - The following is based on my experience and my observation of how Anti-Thoroughbred Racing ecoterrorists operate and what motivates them to carry out their unlawful activities. It is based mainly on my personal experience with one crime group and on material published by this terroristic group – and responses published by other victims.]*

By the time the crime group had put my former employer, Star Barn Thoroughbreds at Agrarian County out of business, I was getting a pretty good handle on how they operate. The alpha leader and "her people" were simply a corrupt organization masquerading as a tax-exempt organization with a perverted charitable cause.

Under close scrutiny, the well-disguised criminal activities were designed to infiltrate and sabotage a Thoroughbred breeding and racing operation with the criminal intent to put the Thoroughbred operation out of business and to take possession of the operation's Thoroughbreds - *all under the guise of official right.* The Thoroughbreds are then distributed as "secret rewards" to members of the crime group from a number of different states.

While committing egregious crimes that are ignored by law enforcement, the psychopathic in-group is able to also fraudulently solicit donations from duped donors and "shamed" former owners, breeders, and trainers.

[* Note - Other perverted animal rights groups use similar tactics and time tested crime schemes. Furthermore, they like to call their undercover ecoterrorists – "undercover investigators" or "authorities"; thus, giving them a veiled pretense of official right.]

[*"To a guilty target the crime scheme may not be all that apparent; however, as an innocent victim the crime scheme is crystal clear." – Paul E. Truitt, DVM"]

[*Please don't take me wrong, there are a lot of good-hearted animal lovers in the world who are genuinely interested in the health, safety, and welfare of animals; that don't make their living by exploiting animals and their caregivers; or, by covertly harming and killing animals to create "shock value" - which is then used to fraudulently solicit donations. Ecoterrorists are *psychopaths* and they do not have the capacity to love other humans - or animals!!!]

When undercover members of the crime group - usurping the power and authority of two well-known national animal rights organizations - coerced Officer Gonzales of the Lebanon County Humane Society and my former boss, Dr. Barr, into euthanizing two healthy mares (knowing that it would leave their foals orphaned) - I knew right then and there that something heinously evil was going on!!!! I had flashbacks of Nashville Animal Control. This was when I figured out that *we were not dealing with a legitimate animal rights group.*

Two years later Dr. Barr informed me about a phone conversation that he had with the alpha leader just prior to the two mares being destroyed; it became apparent that this despicable ploy was an act of *vicious retaliation*; simply because Dr. Barr would not cave in to their extortion attempts to turn the two mares and their foals over to the alpha leader and her people.

Integral Parts of their Signature Crime Scheme:

1. Anti-Thoroughbred Racing ecoterrorists are constantly on the lookout for new targets within the Thoroughbred industry. *Without any legal right or justification*, these corrupt organizations will target and covertly sabotage a Thoroughbred racing and breeding operations.

2. Since "envy and greed" seem to be motivating factors, the first step in their Signature Crime Scheme is to target *well-known* owners, breeders and trainers with *high-quality* Thoroughbreds.

3. If the target has no apparent weaknesses or vulnerabilities, the terrorists will maliciously and covertly create them by

using undercover saboteurs. Since they specialize in exploiting Thoroughbred Racing, the more prominent the target, the greater the *shock value* and more intense the *public outrageous.*

4. These corrupt organizations have infiltrated and have considerable influence and control over the Thoroughbred industry, especially in the Mid-Atlantic states; law enforcement agencies; other non-profit organizations i.e. HSUS, PETA, ASPCA, state and local humane societies, and animal control agencies; public horse auctions; the News Media; Political Groups; and, Thoroughbred race tracks.

5. While ecoterrorists often uses the *"dark side"* of Thoroughbred racing as their veiled political privilege to attack the industry; ***in reality, ecoterrorism is by far the darkest side of Thoroughbred Racing.***

6. The target's employees, clients, business relations, and veterinarians are routinely contacted and solicited by the terrorists to aid and abet the crime group's deceptive and covert criminal activities.

7. These perverted charitable organizations routinely use the owner's employees to secretly sabotage the targeted operations; the criminal intent is to weaken the owner economically, professionally, socially, and emotionally. They will covertly damage and destroy property; including the owners' horses, while making it look accidental.

8. A favored technique of the terrorists is to defame and vilify their targeted victims by spreading *outrageous lies* and questioning the victim's honesty, integrity, trustworthiness, motives, character, competence, skills, sanity, and judgment.

   This signature method is used none stop from start to finish; members of the crime group (from all over the US) will continuously *parrot* the fabricated lies as if they were personal witnesses; until the *insane lies* are perceived as the truth.

9. Out of pure evil – the ecoterrorists *fabricate evidence* to support their outrageous lies about their victims; the terrorists' undercover saboteurs will unconscionably starve, neglect, harm and/or kill the targeted victim's horses.

   As a matter of criminal law, these despicable acts are classified as: aggravated criminal sabotage; aggravated agriculture vandalism; and, aggravated animal cruelty. The aggravated crimes are intended to put the owner out of business and/or to falsely prosecute the owner. This is ecoterrorism at its most evil!!!

10. Ecoterrorists frequently *contact all the owner's clients and other economic relations* to insure that the outrageous lies have reached

them and done their intended harm. This despicable twisted act is aggravated interfere with economic relations.

11. With the intent to maliciously prosecute the targeted owner, members of the crime groups (from all over the US) file numerous false animal abuse reports with various law enforcement agencies. This crime, as a matter of criminal law, is *aggravated false reporting*; those filing the false reports usually have never seen the victim's horses!

12. To compound the damages, members of the crime groups will then *publically parrot the "fabricated fact" - that the owner is under investigation* by numerous law enforcement agencies *for abusing and starving his animals.* This is the aggravated tort of *false light.*

13. With an insane sense of entitlement, the crime group will methodically deprive the owner of their Thoroughbred horses (*under the perverted guise of official right*) by death, theft, coercion, theft by deception, extortion, and exaction; and sometimes, even make the owner pay to get their stolen and/or illegally seized horses back.

14. If forced to return the horses to the owner, the ecoterroristic in-group also demands an outrageous amount of "restitution" for having to *"rescue"* and care for the stolen and/or illegal seized horses.

15. *Shaming* and/or coercing the alleged "rescued" horses' *former owners and trainers into making "donations"* is another common ploy.

16. When allowed, the terrorists *usurp the power and authority of vulnerable law enforcement agencies and race track officials.* This fits a pattern of *racketeering.*

17. By creating the false impression that the owner "sent horses to slaughter" and "starved and abused horses", the well-connected crime groups gets track officials to deny the owner and/or the owner's trainer access to their tracks; thus effectively shutting down the victim's racing operation causing more irreparable harm; which dupes the track officials into aiding and abetting the crime group; and, amounts to more *racketeering.*

18. These criminal acts interfere with the owner's and trainer's right to freely compete at the targeted race tracks; and, violates the owner's and trainer's *right of free competition.*

19. When ecoterrorists are allowed to manipulate law enforce and the Justice System, they will take the owner's Thoroughbreds under

the perverted pretense of official right. This is nothing less than *extortion* and *exaction!*

20. If all else fails, the terrorists will seek out and maliciously *target all the owner's economic relations and repeat their signature crime scheme* with any one doing business with the targeted owner. This is *aggravated tortuous interference with the intent to commit ecoterrorism -* to prevent the target from participating in Thoroughbred breeding and racing.

One perverted tax-exempt organization's "trademark" scam is to target vulnerable public horse auctions and *maliciously mislabels them as "slaughter" or "killer" sales*. These legitimate public sales are legally open to horses of all breeds. There is nothing illegal about these sales. As a matter of fact, they serve as a major market for companion, pleasure, and work horses; especially, Thoroughbreds that have been re-trained as show or pleasure horses. All the sound adult horses at SBT were trained for pleasure riding.

[*Note - I am adamantly against euthanizing or killing healthy animals. As a veterinarian, there were times when owners would ask me to euthanize a health animal; I refused to put healthy animals down; e*xcept, *when I was coerced into euthanizing thousands of healthy animals by corrupt Nashville, TN government officials; this was one of their ways to retaliate against me for exposing their wrongdoing.]*

[*Note: Because of the almost certain negative backlash from animal activist groups, Thoroughbred owners and trainers would never sell a horse intended for slaughter at one of these targeted auctions. In fact, if an owner was not opposed to slaughtering horses for animal or human consumption, they would send them directly to a buyer or processing plant without paying any consignment fees or commissions that often exceeds the purchase price for horses that are brought for food.]

The "Sent to Slaughter Scam" goes like this:

1. Since these terrorists specialize in exploiting the Thoroughbred industry, they *only target identifiable Thoroughbreds* at the targeted public auctions.

2. When a member of the crime group identifies any Thoroughbred that is consigned to one of the targeted public auctions, they *create the false impression that the horse was "sent to slaughter" or "sent to a kill pen"*.

3. If a Thoroughbred is of *high-quality*, a member of the crime group will purchase the horse; then, *create the false impression that the purchased horse was "rescued" from a "kill pen"*.

4. Members of the crime group then *fraudulently solicit public donations* to care for high-quality Thoroughbreds that are *privately purchased and owned* by members of the crime group by misrepresenting the horses as "rescued".

5. The ecoterrorists also *maliciously seek out and exploit the previous owners, trainers, and breeders* of Thoroughbreds consigned to the targeted auctions.

6. Previous owners, trainers, and breeders are thoroughly *investigated* by members of the crime group to find possible weak points and/or useful private information.

7. A highly effective method used by the crime group is to exploit previous owners, trainers, and breeders by *"shaming" and/or coercing them into making donations* to members that operate perverted *tax-exempt* organizations.

8. If a previous owner or trainer refuses to support the terrorists with coerced donations, the crime group *will retaliate by carrying out their signature crime scheme with the owner* or trainer as the primary target, as described above.

In one well-known *hoax/scam*, donations were fraudulently solicited for over 2 years **after** a group of Thoroughbreds in Ohio had already been placed in new homes. "In Urgent Need of Placement - 52 Thoroughbreds going to slaughter on Saturday" was the crime group's fraudulent outcry for donations. *Donations were sent as far away as Great Britain.* **The truth was that the horses had already been placed by the deceased owner and his family before the scam was ever created!**

Star Barn Thoroughbreds at Agrarian Country was forced out of business on Oct. 28th of 2011.

The ecoterrorists were still using the "Star Barn Scam" in June of 2014 to fraudulently solicit donations.

[See the June 2014 edition of the *PENNSYLVANIA EQUESTRIAN* *"THE NEWS HORSE OWNERS NEED TO KNOW"* The Star Barn Saga: 'Get Rich' Scheme Cost Dozens of Horses' Lives by Amy Wooden]

CHAPTER 10

Summary of Their Mode of Operation

In the United States, the *Organized Crime Control Act* (1970) defines organized crime as "The unlawful activities of [...] a highly organized, disciplined association [...]".

Anti-Thoroughbred Racing terrorists are well-organized crime groups masked as Thoroughbred rescue operations and/or as tax-exempt organizations with noble causes; one crime group's published purpose is to rescue Thoroughbred horses from slaughter. However, under close scrutiny, their published words, coupled with their actions, reveal that their hidden agenda is meant to exploit targeted Thoroughbred owners, trainers, and breeders – the Thoroughbred industry in general.

Although these terroristic crime groups would like for the public to view them as anti-Thoroughbred Racing animal rights activists; and that their ultimate goal is to "see the demise of Thoroughbred Racing" - that is not their true agenda.

Their real agenda is to fraudulently solicit donations by creating shocking situations that will outrageous the public and bring in the donations. In reality, they *create* and feed off the dark side of Thoroughbred Racing.

These terroristic crime groups target: vulnerable owners and trainers with *high-quality* Thoroughbreds; affluent former owners and breeders who can be *coerced or shamed* into making donations; law enforcement agencies and race tracks who will allow terrorists to usurp their power and authority; veterinarians and employees who are willing to betray their employers for personal gain; News Media personnel that looks for perverted *stories that will shock and outrage the public* - rather than seeking the truth; and, members of the general public who can be duped by insane lies and conned into making donations.

By her own admission, the alpha leader of one of the terroristic crime groups and "her people" have infiltrated and have considerable control over: the Thoroughbred Industry; law enforcement agencies; other non-profit organizations; public horse auctions; the News Media; and, vulnerable Thoroughbred race tracks.

These ecoterrorists have a signature mode of operation (crime scheme), which includes: (a) sabotaging the targeted owner's Thoroughbred operate causing the owner severe economic, social, professional, and emotional distress; (b) vilifying the victim by parroting malicious and insane allegations meant to defame, shame, blame, and frame the targeted owner; (c) fabricating evidence against the targeted owner by maliciously harming the target's horses or putting them in harm's way; (d) continually filing false reports; (e) continually stalking and harassing the targeted owner; (f) maliciously prosecuting the owner by fabricating charges of animal cruelty, abuse, starvation, etc.; (g) interfering with all the target's business relations; (h) taking the targeted owner's Thoroughbreds under the perverted pretense of official right by usurping the power and authority of duped and manipulated law enforcement agencies; and, depriving the owner of the use of their Thoroughbreds by harm, death, coercion, or by theft by deception, extortion, and exaction.

After being continually stalked and targeted by these people, it became obvious to me that *they were not legitimate animal lovers*. I knew from their actions that they had evil intentions; and, as a victim, *I knew their outrageous lies were insane.* Therefore, I started to thoroughly research the type of behavior that I was observing. *It quickly became obvious that the behavior of ecoterrorists fit the psychological profile of psychopaths.*

CHAPTER 11

The Theory of the Star Barn Case

As a matter of law, the ecoterrorists had absolutely no privilege or right to infringe on or to deprive Star Barn Thoroughbreds at Agrarian County (my former employer) of their: funding; contract rights; business relations; clients; track earnings; PA breeders' awards; and, PA owners awards. Star Barn Thoroughbreds was the Equine Division of Agrarian Country's Proposed International School of Agriculture.

Why would a perverted non-profit group that was based in California and a corrupt in-group of government employees from Nashville, TN so insanely target my new employer when I moved from Nashville, TN to Grantville, PA to manage a Thoroughbred operation; especially since, the new PA Thoroughbred operation was formed for charitable, educational, and research purposes?

The answer is simple: The corrupt Nashville government officials were still *insanely obsessed* with destroying my livelihood; they were not going to let me move to another state and work unmolested. Due to their psychopathic nature, they did not want me to practice veterinary medicine in *any* state or have anything to do with animals. They knew how much I loved animals of all kinds; and, they insanely wanted to take that away from me for no other reason than I had exposed their wrongdoing in Nashville.

Making contact and conspiring with the psychopathic alpha leader of a terroristic crime group in PA was the ideal way for the tyrants from Nashville to continue their relentless retaliation again me. After talking with the Nashville ring leader, the terroristic crime leader from California had to perceive me as a serious threat to her illegal activities in PA. Furthermore, the ecoterrorists also saw an opportunity to exploit millions of dollars' worth of assets from my new employer, Agrarian Country, who had been approved for a grant of $155 million to establish its International School of Agriculture and Expo Center.

In retrospect, the most probable cause that Agrarian Country was targeted by the anti-Thoroughbred ecoterrorists from its beginning was that *the terrorists were already established and in control of the Thoroughbred farm* when Agrarian Country leased it from the widows of two previous Thoroughbred owners – two men who were mysteriously killed in an unsolved helicopter crash in 2006.

The fact that Dr. Barr hired me to manage the new operator was a threat to the terrorists' established management control of that operation. So the ecoterrorists did what psychopaths do, they tried to dig up dirt on me; so they made contact with the Nashville group after doing a background check.

Even though, I had been exonerated of all the fabricated charges brought against me by the Nashville coconspirators, the ecoterrorists use those old fabricated lies once again to maliciously vilify me. Ecoterrorists know that if you parrot lies enough times, many will start to believe them; and, many others won't care either way.

Perception is all that matters to corrupt government officials, terrorists, and psychopaths. Their first step was to try to get Dr. Barr to believe the despicable lies about me. When that did not work, they parroted the lies on the Internet and maliciously communicated them to all the Star Barn clients and business associates.

The ecoterrorists also had an insane envy and hatred of all the good things that Agrarian Country had planned. That envy and hatred grew even more after Star Barn Thoroughbreds had rebuilt the Thoroughbred operation; greed and an insane sense of entitlement to the Star Barn horses took over. Even though some of the undercover saboteurs had a bright future at Star Barn Thoroughbreds - far better than what awaits them now – they had enough evil in their souls to inspire them to side with the terrorists.

Now they may be facing up to 40 years in prison and a statutory fine of up to $250,000. They also face playing treble the damages done; which is mandated no matter what their economic situation.

It is a shame that some of the most talented and trusted SBT employees laid waste to their futures by aiding and abetting the criminal activities of the seasoned ecoterrorists.

To my detriment, I had a history of recognizing and standing up to those who misuse their power and authority to unconscionably harm others. I now see that this is my fate. With the Spirit of Good guiding and directing me, I was well-prepared to fight this lop-sided battle – experienced and well-educated in the right areas.

My good nature and my need to do what is right naturally motivate me to first ask the wrongdoers to correct the situation. This usually works when dealing with somewhat normal people; however, some of those that I exposed have a psychopathic tendency to relentlessly retaliate against anyone who does not affirm their deceptive and coercive practices. The root of my problems can be traced as far back to the spring of 1998; to the Director of the Health Relation Boards in Nashville, TN.

The well-established ecoterrorists knew my background well. The corrupt organization recognized me as an individual with strong moral and ethical values; someone who does not tolerate wrongdoing. I was a definite threat to the ecoterrorists!!

Who would think that strong work ethics and doing the right thing would cause a person so much grief? It is not new; since the beginning of history, good people have been targeted by the evil-spirited. Tyrants insanely feel that no one has the right to questions their deviant power or authority or to interfere with their illegal or immoral schemes, they detest and retaliate against those who do not approve of them and affirm their perverted behavior.

I was much hated in Tennessee for "bucking their (corrupt) system"; in other words, I was hated for exposing a corrupt system that had used its powers and authority for years to exploit those they were supposed to be serving and protecting.

Consequently, I decided to move to Pennsylvania to get away from the hostile Nashville environment. But much to my chagrin, the Tennessee coconspirators had beaten me to PA; they had contacted, or had been contacted by, the leader of the ecoterrorists.

The continuing conspiracy was simple and clear - intimidate, harass, coerce, and stalk Dr. Truitt; and, interfere with Dr. Truitt's business relationships; the criminal objectives were to prevent Dr. Truitt from practicing veterinary medicine and/or to prevent him from participating in the Thoroughbred Industry. This was nothing short of ecoterrorism – as defined by the statutes of Pennsylvania!

I had to learn the hard way, so I must stress the fact that *it is important to understand how to recognize psychopaths, tyrants, and/or terrorists.* They show no compassion or mercy! Many of the methods used by ecoterrorists to destroy my career and business relations are highly characteristic of psychopathic behavior. Like most victims, I did not realize the magnitude of what was going on in PA until I was beaten down to the point that I was yet again economically "disabled". Without any protection from law enforcement and without the economic resources to pursue it civilly, I had to just roll with the punches and to let them have their way with me - and my horses!!

Whereas the terroristic group in Nashville targeted pet stores and the store's employees, the group in PA targeted Thoroughbred owners, breeders, and trainers. Like most terroristic groups, someone usually comes forward to take the credit after the plan has been successfully carried out!! The alpha leader from California/Great Britain claimed that "honor" by posting – "Finally, Pennsylvania and Thoroughbred racing in general are rid of the good Dr. Truitt."

CHAPTER 12

SBT Targeted from the Beginning to End

Although I first felt that the farm in Grantville, PA was "cursed". *In reality, it was not cursed; it had been covertly sabotaged from its beginning to its end; just like its predecessor, Regal Heir Farm. This secret was a closely guarded by the hidden ecoterrorists!!*

When Dr. Barr leased the farm in Oct. 2009, the alpha leader of the domestic terrorists already had "her people" in place; they were former employees of the failed Regal Heir Farm / Pennsylvania Horse Farms, LLC operations.

In October of 2009, Agrarian Country, a 501 (c) (3) non-profit organization, Dr. Robert Barr, president, leased the farm formerly known as Regal Heir Farm from Pennsylvania Horse Farms, LLC in Grantville, PA. Other large tracts of prime farm land adjacent to the old Regal Heir Farm had been contracted by Dr. Barr for a very ambitious project - Agrarian County and its International School of Agriculture and Expo Center.

The entire Agrarian Country Project was very exciting to me – and many others. I loved farming and animals of all kinds. I especially loved Thoroughbred racing and breeding. The plan included an International Agricultural Center, featuring all facets of agriculture. The idea was well received in the area. The "Farm Show" in nearby Harrisburg was one of the biggest annual events in PA. Literally millions attended the event each year; Agrarian Country was to be a year-round agriculture exposition and education center. It had so many "good" things planned!

After months of responding to numerous false and malicious complaints of animal cruelty from the terroristic crime group, the Lebanon County Humane Society never found any cause to charge Dr. Barr or SBT - primarily because I had voluntarily intervened when the undercover ecoteurs intentional harmed or failed to take proper care of the horses. As a volunteer - and for a number of months - I unknowingly kept foiling the terrorists' plans.

However, within two years, the Agrarian Country Projects had been maliciously destroyed by undercover terrorists. We barely knew what had hit us!

On Oct. 28, 2011, Dr. Barr informed me that Star Barn Thoroughbreds at Agrarian County was officially going out of business and that he was donating the few remaining Agrarian Country horses to our Charitable Trust. Furthermore, on Oct. 28, 2011, Dr. Barr resigned his role as Trustee of the Charitable Trust, leaving me as the sole Trustee. Dr. Barr had been "'sucker punched" by an invisible evil force!!

The really disturbing thing was that once we had figured out what had happened - there was absolutely no "equal protection under the law". The egregious terroristic acts of the crime group were simply ignored by the Lebanon County Justice System; the State Police; the FBI; the PA Attorney General, Kathleen Kane; and, the US Attorney General, Eric Holder.

[*Over a period of fifteen years, the terrorists methodically destroyed all my business relations and deprived the beneficiaries of my Charitable Trusts of all its high-quality Thoroughbred horses; and, its tangible and intangible assets. The actual damages just to the Trust and me are estimated to be over $40 million. The collateral damages are many times that amount. Of all my business relations, Star Barn Thoroughbreds at Agrarian Country was perhaps the most prized and esteemed of all!]

CHAPTER 13

What Really Happened to SBT?

Trusting and altruistic people like Dr. Barr and I were easy targets for the undercover master deceivers and manipulators. Psychopaths rarely have difficulty with the law, because they seek out situations where their tyrannical behavior will be tolerated, condoned, or even admired. *What better "mask" could ecoterrorists have than masquerading as charitable organizations with noble causes?*

The ecoterrorists and their undercover accomplices knew that Pennsylvania *ignores and fails to enforce* their ecoterrorism and agriculture vandalism laws. And because they were *masked as animal rights activists* and had people working undercover at the farm and with law enforcement, they knew that their criminal activities would go unpunished; and even be admired!

While employed as the general manager of SBT at AC from Jan. 2010 until Nov. of 2010. I was continually challenged by the passive aggressive behavior of the paid SBT undercover saboteurs. Being an honest and trusting person, I perceived their aberrant behavior as a lack of work ethics, insubordination, dishonesty, incompetence and/or just plan laziness – *"ecoterrorism"* never crosses my mind.

Aggravated criminal sabotage, aggravated agriculture vandalism, and aggravated animal cruelty with the criminal intent to commit ecoterrorism were made to appear as accidents!!!

It all actually started as soon as I was interviewed by Dr. Barr for the management position at Agrarian County. I met two of the undercover ecoterrorists when I came to the farm with Dr, Barr in October of 2009.

I found out later that they had tried to discourage Dr. Barr from hiring me by falsely claiming that my license to practice veterinary medicine in Tennessee had been revoked and that I had several counts of abuse on my record. Since that time these two *despicable lies* have been *parroted* by the terroristic crime group.

That was just the beginning!

[*Of course it was a closely guard secret that Star Bar had been targeted from the start. I did not find out until almost 3 years later – a year after SBT had been forced out of business.]

When I moved to the farm in January of 2010, I got a very cold reception from the farm staff, former employees of Regal Heir Farm/Pennsylvania Thoroughbred Farms, LLC. First, they refused to help my wife and I unload our furniture from the U-Haul that I had just driven for over 17 hours in a blinding snow storm. It was not until Dr. Barr send out some of the staff from the main office in Middletown, PA did anyone at the farm lift a hand. I now assume that they did secretly lift a finger!!

From the start, the staff was outwardly resistant to my recommendations to improve the care that the horses at the farm were receiving. Dr. Barr was called to the farm on a couple of occasions to mediate when they refused. It was not long until the arrogant and/or intentional insubordination of the farm's managers and foaling personnel caused the death of a valuable foal - the mare's previous foal by a lesser stallion sold for $400,000 at public auction later that year.

Soon thereafter, the entire farm staff failed to show up for work one morning. Much to their dismay, I took care of all the horses myself. When three of them showed up late that afternoon, I fired a couple of them for insubordination and/or (intentional) gross incompetence – my two biggest stressors! The third employee quit before I could fire her. I still remember how those two undercover saboteurs got extremely fowl-mouthed and went head-spinning ballistic *just before* I terminated their employment!!!

Soon thereafter, the entire staff failed to show up for work again. I fired the remaining manager and 2 two other staff members who turned out to be illegal aliens. All six of those employees are now believed to have been working undercover for the ecoterrorists.

This must have infuriated the entire group of covert ecoterrorists; because, firing those six ecoteurs messed up their undercover control of the operation for the next several months.

As an integral part of their signature crime scheme, the undercover crime group retaliated and began to defame SBT and me by maliciously and falsely claiming that *I had fired the entire SBT staff*; that *all the horses at SBT had been turned out to fend for themselves*; and, that *all the elite stallions were turned out with the mares to breed unattended.* In reality, we still had around 10 employees to take care of only twenty some odd horses.

Furthermore, the undercover ecoterrorists immediately contacted all the stallion owners and other SBT clients to insure that their outrageous lies had reached each and every one of them. This was enough to cast a false light on the new operation. Not only did it hurt Star Barn Thoroughbreds, the criminal activities of the group would later cause the stallion owners a lot of damages in lost stallion awards.

Since I had just fired 3 key management employees, I naturally thought that all this was "sour grapes". Ecoterrorism still had not crossed my mind.

During that first year, the pre-approved, politically-backed funding for Agrarian County was continually delayed; finally, it was threatened that it would all be withdrawn in its entirety - unless the funding for the Thoroughbred division was "excluded" from the general plan; which I dismissed simply as being very odd! I now believed - that the far-reaching, politically-charged crime group interfered with the entire $155 million funding process; not just the $5.5 million that was to go to the Thoroughbred operation.

Even though, we were being silently sabotaged for the entire first year of our operation and deprived of the expected funding; we had rebuilt the operation into an 80+ horse operation with an outstanding 2011 foal crop of 42 expected soon. We had also picked up several new clients.

Even undercover members of the crime group (posing as clients and members of the News Media) seemed to be impressed with what we had done to rebuild the operation; an operation that had previously gone from a leading Thoroughbred operation (Regal Heir Farm) with as many as 200 horses down to a failing operation with only 17 horses productive horses and a few non-paying horses that had been "rescued" by the terminated saboteurs. Judging from the unexplained decline of its operation, I suspect that Regal Heir had also been sabotaged, prior to Dr. Barr leasing the farm. I was not informed until almost a year after SBT had been forced out of business - that some of the staff retained from Regal Heir had been working with the alpha leader of the ecoterrorists from the start of the SBT operation.

We successfully restored the Thoroughbred operation to an impressive level; even though it was still being undermined by the terrorists; however, once the funding had been withdrawn, SBT was forced to make cut-backs on staff and horses.

It also appears that it was not just the undercover employees that were working with the ecoterrorists. What I now believed that undercover members of the group (posing as clients) boarded horses at the farm; breed their mares to farm stallions; had us train their horses up to being almost ready to race; and, then they intentionally refused to paid; thus, adding to the economic duress. Over $200,000 worth of breeding, boarding, and training services was drained from the operation in that matter.

Still desperately wanting the entire Agrarian County operation to succeed, I volunteered to be laid-off in November of 2010. *Ironically, so that 4 or 5 paid undercover saboteurs could keep their jobs!*

[*Perceptions and false impressions are all that matter to psychopaths; they are not in touch with Reality and the Truth.]*

This literally "opened the doors, fences, and gates" for the *stealthy* ecoterrorists. One of their signature terroristic acts was to open stall doors, barn doors, and gates and to tear down 16' sections of perimeter fence so that horses were able to get out and off the farm; thus putting the horses and vehicle operators on the adjacent highways and expressway at risk of catastrophic and potentially fatal accidents. This became my biggest nightmare!!

After I was laid-off, Dr. Barr assumed the responsibilities of the general management from his office in Middletown, PA and full-time paid employees (including undercover saboteurs) were assigned specific management positions and the duties and responsibilities of those positions at SBT. Both undercover employees and undercover clients are now believed to have played major roles in the sabotage of Star Barn Thoroughbreds.

As fate would have it - I was unknowingly still a thorn in the side of the ecoterrorists. I had been retained as a part-time advisor; therefore, I repeatedly reminded the paid managing employees of their duties and responsibilities to no avail. *Insanely*, the undercover saboteurs (and their off-farm coconspirators) continued to *blame* me for their own nonfeasance and malfeasance; when in fact, *they were ignorantly incriminating themselves!*

Must to their dismay, I continued to voluntarily performed tasks that paid undercover employees failed to do; thus, unknowingly mitigating the effects of the intentional wrongdoing of the paid saboteurs. Theft of tools, feed, and supplies became commonplace. The destruction of farm equipment and harm to the horses were masterfully made to appear as accidents.

It was not until the undercover saboteurs had helped the outside terrorists put SBT out of business and then came out of hiding that I started putting all the pieces together; most despicable of all, many of the horses belonging to SBT, the Trust, and clients were the victims of aggravated animal cruelty at the hands of the undercover saboteurs.

What were once thought to be "accidents" were obviously terroristic acts. Dark sinister things had been done to the horses!!!! At least 4 (and as many as 10) horses were shot or speared in or near their private parts; what appeared to be puncture wounds or acute cases of severe colic, abortion, and/or complications from foaling; were in fact caused by despicable signature acts of brutality. At least six horses received life ending injuries.

Another one of the signature criminal acts was to give mares prostaglandins, a drug which first caused them to appear to have a mild case of colic; however, soon thereafter the mares would often abort their foals.

I also voluntarily trained horses for SBT until May 15, 2011; at which time SBT suspended its racing operation when it became obvious that the racing operation was being sabotaged and someone was trying to frame me for "doping" horses.

Without any potential earning from racing, by June of 2011, the saboteurs had weakened SBT to the point that Dr. Barr was forced to sell several horses at a public Thoroughbred auction and privately.

Even though, SBT no longer owned the subject horses, some of them showed up at a couple of the group's targeted public auctions. This opened the door for the crime group's trademark scam – the "rescued from slaughter" and "rescued from kill pens" scam; which are used to vilify the owners and to "fraudulently soliciting public donations" - to care for privately purchased and owned horses.

As an integral part of this signature crime scheme, the crime group maliciously and falsely published that SBT had sent horses to "slaughter" and that members of the crime group had rescued them from "kill pens".

After that, the far-reaching crime group continually and publically parroted these outrageous lies; the success of their crime scheme was partially made possible by continually vilifying Dr. Barr and me by creating and reinforcing numerous false impressions.

After covertly sabotaging SBT for 20 continuous months and then outrageously vilifying Dr. Barr and me, in July of 2011, the terroristic crime group intensified their aggravated criminal behavior. Members of the crime group maliciously contacted SBT clients yet again to make sure that the group's outrageous lies had reached them, causing most of the remaining clients to move their horses. Furthermore, if the horses were not moved, they were covertly harmed or killed by undercover ecoteurs.

In late June and early July 2011, I started getting hate calls and emails at all hours of the day and night insanely accusing me of sending horses to slaughter. Dr. Barr and I also received veiled threats; such as, "how are these men still standing?" "Why have they not been prosecuted?" "They ought to be in jail." "Mr. Paul Truitt should be HUNG" and "I will see that approach is carried out".

Since the group was able to "dupe" a lot of people into making public donations with the outrageous "sent to slaughter" and "rescued from kill pens" scam, the terrorists began to fabricate and parrot more egregious lies about Dr. Barr and me; such as, "SBT horses are being starved and abused." And "Dr. Barr and Dr. Truitt defrauded the owners who donated horses and capital."

Of course, the old stand-by outrageous lies that my license to practice in TN had been revoked because of animal abuse was also frequently and maliciously reinforced. On one occasion, a false report was filed with the Pennsylvanian Bureau of Investigations; and, I was investigated. Even though the allegations "that I was practicing veterinary medicine without a license" were found to be absolutely false by the two investigating officers, the "infiltrated" main office of the PBI continued to threaten me by making sure that I knew that the investigation "was not closed" and "would be ongoing".

The crime of false reporting was ignored yet again; thus, facilitating and/or compounding the ecoterrorism; and, *empowering the terrorists to act uninhibited by law enforcement.*

Revealing the crime group's ulterior motive and criminal intent - on July 7, 2011, the alpha leader informed Dr. Barr that she and "her people" intended to put SBT out of business and take all the SBT horses. And that she and "her people" would not stop at *anything* until that happened.

The alpha leader also insanely attempted to coerce Dr. Barr into firing me; even though, I had been laid-off since November of 2010. She was obviously angered because I was voluntarily foiling many of their continual attempts to sabotage the SBT operation.

The alpha leader must have been sure that her attempt to extort the SBT horses would be successful, because she and "her people" set up a Facebook page, "Star Barn Thoroughbreds – Broodmares Need Urgent Placement". This was similar to the scam pulled off in Ohio – "52 Thoroughbreds Need Urgent Placement – Going to Slaughter on Saturday"; except, the Ohio horses had already been placed before the group began fraudulently solicited donations.

*The noteworthy difference in the two scams was that in the Star Bar Scam - *the alleged "sent to slaughter" and "rescued" horses had never left the farm.*

Once again, the ecoterrorists maliciously called numerous clients of SBT and the previous owners and breeders of horses at SBT and falsely stated that SBT was starving and abusing their horses and that the remaining horses were in urgent need of placement. Consequently, all but two of the paying clients moved their horses causing SBT even more economic duress.

> [*Note - The terrorists later killed one of the remaining client's 3 month old foal by rupturing her rectum; and, they attempted to kill the other client's stallion, It's So Simple, by mutilating his feet with a pair of hoof nippers.]

Looking back – the ecoterrorists targeted SBT client horses until they were either dead or moved from the farm. In many cases, a client's vet bills to treat injured horses were higher that the board bills – as with two client mares treated by an undercover vet.

After being able to create the false impression that Star Barn was sending horses to slaughter, some of the terrorists masked as "animal activists" came out from under their cover. The ecoterrorists continually defamed, harassed, coerced, and vilified Dr. Barr and me by publically parroting their outrageous lies. Their perverted social network had been specifically set-up for that purpose. Ironically, the members of the group were only incriminating themself by going public with their criminal intentions to commit ecoterrorism as defined by PA law – put Star Barn out of business.

These insane people misled many to believe that they had "rescued from slaughter" the horses on their published lists of SBT and Trust horses; and that they had the legal right and authority to give the horses away; or, return them to the alleged defrauded previous owners. People, *posing as* previous owners, were showing up at the farm unannounced with their horse trailers to pick up "their" horses. Some were caught trespassing as they arrogantly went out into the pastures to take horses. In Reality, there were no "defrauded previous owners" and none of the horses had ever left the farm or been sent to slaughter.

Ironically, it was self-incriminating - *and very ignorant* - for the undercover paid saboteurs to claim that horses were being abused and/or starved at SBT; since, they were the same *paid* SBT employees responsible for the care and safety of the horses.

Furthermore, the psychopaths/terrorists were unable to comprehend that my wife and I were altruistically volunteering our time and could not be held culpable for the egregious acts of agriculture vandalism and aggravated animal cruelty directed at my *former* employer and us. *Psychopaths just can't wrap their evil little ignorant minds around "altruism";* "helping others without expecting anything in return" is far beyond their comprehension!

One anonymous undercover ecoterrorist called me a plethora of names heavily laced with profanity for volunteering my time and other resources; stating that he just could not believe that anyone would be f*****g crazy enough to do that.

As most terrorists do, it is now obvious that the alpha leader fully expected Dr. Barr to cave in on her demands: that he must get out of the Thoroughbred business; that he must turn over all the SBT horses to her and "her people"; *and,* that he must get rid of me. Although the group stretched out over several states and Great Britain, only a hand full of the terrorists (besides the undercover employees and clients) ever visited SBT and saw the horses in person.

The few undercover terrorists that came to the farm did see how well cared for the STB horses were. Yet they still reinforced the outrageous lies that the horses were being starved and abused. This was probably due to the fact that they had an unknown advantage over Dr. Barr and me; they secretly knew that their undercover saboteurs would probably succeed in harming the horses and that their *sick self-filling prophesy* would probably come true sooner or later. Like in the movies – framing the good guys is a common devious act used by villains.

Exhibiting a *psychopathic sense of entitlement* to the SBT horses, on July 13, 2011, a member of the crime group posted entire lists of Star Barn horses on their Facebook page, stating, "STB broodmares that need placement as soon as possible." "STB yearlings that need placement as soon as possible." "SBT weanlings that need placement as soon as possible." "SBT sent to slaughter 6/27/11"

> *An undisputable fact is that – not a single horse on the ecoterrorists' published lists had been sent to slaughter; in fact, they had never left the farm!!* [*False perceptions are all that matter to psychopaths/ terrorists/corrupt government officials; the Truth and Orders of the Court are "irrelevant".]

Even though SBT had an open visitation policy and put several of its horses up for adoption, not a single one of the Facebook listed horses were ever adopted or placed by any of the terrorists.

I had given one of the terrorists (posing as a journalist) a complete tour of the farm earlier, then she and her assistant did an article on the farm. They seemed to be impressed with what we were doing; ironically, our success only gave the terrorists more assets to steal.

The member of the crime group - that posted the entire lists of Star Barn and Trust horses - later came to the farm posing as someone interested in adopting one of the mares and her foal. As with a continual flow of visitors who got a personal tour of the farm, she commented to me that the mare seemed to be a lot fatter and healthier than she expected; and, that the foal (alleged by her group to be "starving and deformed") was a picture of health – and that she could not see any deformity to the foal's legs. Being required to sign an adoption contract foiled her ploy to take that mare and foal. Why sign a contract when your group was planning to just take the horses under the perverted pretense of official right as soon as they could get Dr. Barr convicted of animal cruelty?

[*I named that foal, "Lilybug", after one of my granddaughters. Sadly the terrorists, knowing that she was one of my favorites, put the "mark of death" on her; she later died of neglect after being illegally seized and disposed of by the terrorists; while the ecoterrorists were being aided and abetted by the Adams County SPCA and their undercover members in that organization.]

It soon became obvious that finding good homes for horses was only the group's false facade; their real motive and intent was to take only high-quality Thoroughbreds by theft by deception. Furthermore, the entire list of targeted horses were misrepresented as "SBT sent to slaughter 6/27/11" - obviously to fraudulently solicit donations to care for so called "rescued" horses.

Things really got ugly after Dr. Barr refused to transfer all the SBT and Trust horses over to the alpha leader and "her people". By now I was starting to figure out what the group was up to; however, the last thing that I expected was the inhumane things that started happening to the targeted horses; which shed light on several past incidences; things that I once thought was just accidents.

At this point, I still did not think that any of the staff was working with the terrorists. They even signed statements to that effect. Furthermore, I never thought that the "animal activists" would insanely harm or kill our horses. I had seen animals wrongfully seized in Nashville. And I had figured out that the group in PA was fraudulently soliciting donations - but I had never imagines that they would harm and kill animals with the intent to frame Dr. Barr!

Soon after the alpha leader specifically demanded that Dr. Barr turn over the mares, My Lucky Number and California Love, the crime group's true colors came through. Facilitated by a couple of big league animal activist groups, they despicably retaliated against Dr. Barr by threatening to prosecute him for animal cruelty *if he did not immediately euthanize the mares.* This act of "terrorism" left the mares' two young foals orphaned. I knew right then-and-there just how insanely evil this group was!

*In retrospect, during the entire time SBT was in existence - as an integral part of their signature crime scheme - covert saboteurs had been intentionally harming horses under their care with the intent to maliciously prosecute Dr. Barr and me for animal cruelty.

It is now obvious that the group's aggravated animal cruelty was intended also to cause both economic and emotional duress; and, to coerce Dr. Barr into surrendering the horses to the terrorists.

Near the end of SBT - judging from her hostile and unprofessional behavior - a vet employed by SBT was solicited by the ecoterrorists to play a role in the criminal conspiracy to put SBT out of business and to extort the SBT horses. By now the group was openly hostile and arrogant!

I must point out that at no time were the undercover saboteurs not provided with hay, feed, and pastures for the horses. At no time where the undercover saboteurs denied needed medication for the horses, except for the time that the undercover vet (under a legal veterinarian-client-patient obligation to SBT) intentionally failed to treat a couple of the SBT weanlings under her care. Instead, the undercover vet tried to coerce and harass SBT into turning the horses over to the ecoterrorists. When that did not happen, she filed a complaint with the Lebanon County Humane Society.

I brought the needed medication from another vet and treated the weanlings myself; they were fully recovered when the vet returned - three weeks later. That time, the undercover vet along with the Lebanon County Humane Society showed up unannounced. The vet was self-appointed to investigate her own false complaint. This is the most unprofessional thing that I have ever seen a veterinarian do!

The undercover vet's connection with the terrorists became more and more obvious as time went by. Finally, I objected to her obvious harassment and confronted the vet. She nonchalantly admitted that the alpha leader had contacted her vet clinic.

Even after SBT had been forced out of business, the undercover vet and the undercover SBT weanling manger continued to play their despicable roles. Ironically, the alpha leader later publicly criticized both of them for "not doing their jobs well"; because, they had not been able to get Dr. Barr and me prosecuted for animal cruelty!!!

Ironically, as a matter of law, the undercover vet and the undercover weanling manager were culpable for the health, safety and welfare of the weanlings; the very weanlings that they were covertly accusing SBT and me of starving and abusing. Furthermore, "greed" backfired on the undercover vet and absolutely proved that the SBT horses were neither sick nor starved; all the unnecessary and expensive blood tests done by the vet came back normal; absolute proof that the SBT weanlings were not starved.

Subsequently, that information was concealed from the Court in Adams County; after 8 weanlings had been illegally seized by the Adams County SPCA; and, the Court had ordered them to be returned.

Back to the terrorists - After the undercover terrorists started to falsely accusing me of sending SBT horses to slaughter, undercover members of the crime group at Penn National Race Track deprived me of my privileges to train or race horses at Penn National Race Track. This forced me to give up all the horses that I was voluntarily training for Star Thoroughbreds; and, for one of the undercover/non-paying clients. This killed SBT's hopes of capitalizing on over a year of getting several horses ready to race.

At that time, ten Agrarian County horses-in-training were donated to our Charitable Trust. On behalf of the Trust, I leased them and seven Trust yearlings to Joe Moriarty, a Thoroughbred trainer from California. It only took the terrorists a few days to attack and destroyed this mutually beneficial relationship; thus, causing Moriarty to abandon the horses after only 8 days in his possession.

All of a sudden, Moriarty knew more about me than I knew about myself. He even threatened to file a report with the Humane Society, if I did not let him out of the contracts.

After two years of sabotaging SBT, the terrorists finally took Dr. Barr down. On Oct. 28, 2011, Dr. Barr informed me that Star Barn Thoroughbreds was officially going out of business and that he was transferring ownership of the few remaining Agrarian Country horses to the Trust.

After months of responding to numerous false reports of animal cruelty from the ecoterrorists, the Lebanon County Humane Society never found any cause to charge Star Barn Thoroughbreds or Dr. Barr; primarily because, I had been voluntarily intervening whenever the undercover SBT saboteurs failed to take proper care of the horses. Subsequently, the ecoterrorists continually defamed and harassed the Lebanon County Humane Society for not letting them usurp its power and authority.

Also on Oct. 28, 2011, Dr. Barr resigned his role as Trustee of SBTBT-A, leaving me as the sole Trustee. Agrarian Country forfeited its beneficial interest in the Trust. Even though the Trust had lost its most important supporter, SBT at Agrarian Country, I felt that I had a continual moral and legal obligation to the beneficiaries of the Charitable Trust. Subsequently, I transferred Agrarian Country's interests in the Trust to Collin's Classic for Kids with Cancer; St. Jude Children's Research Hospital; and, the Make-A-Wish Foundation.

Besides the death of one's eternal soul, working for a group of terrorists has predictable consequences. When their plan to falsely prosecute Dr. Barr and me failed, the alpha leader and "her people" began publicizing that the solicited vet did not do her job well. For not standing up for what was just and good from the beginning, the undercover vet's career and soul was basically destroyed.

A number of other duped accomplices, including the weanling manager and an undercover coconspirator, who were posing as my friends, confidants, and business affiliate - also later experienced the psychopathic wrath of the alpha leader and her "people".

Back to the deadly sin of Greed - The excessive and unnecessary blood work done by the undercover vet was Dr. Barr's saving grace; it only proved that the horses at Star Barn Thoroughbreds were normal and healthy. It obviously frustrated and angered the undercover terrorists when their attempts to falsely incriminate and prosecute Dr. Barr failed.

As you will see later, *any* (duped or willing) accomplice who fails to carry out their end of the "conspiratorial bargain" with the terrorists always suffers the wrath of alpha leader.

If not for me continuously intervening and reminding the paid saboteurs of their duties and responsibilities and often doing their neglected jobs for them, there certainly would have been horses starved and neglected at Star Barn Thoroughbreds. And since I had not been a paid employee of SBT for almost a year, they could not hold me culpable for their undercover saboteurs' nonfeasance and malfeasance. That left the paid undercover saboteurs culpable – and a couple of their psychopathic leaders "head-spinning ballistic".

If not for my altruism as a volunteer, the horses would have unknowingly been at the mercy of the ecoterrorists; if not for me voluntarily intervening, the animal victims of the group's aggravated animal cruelty would not have received pain relief and proper treatment. Nor would the egregious actions of the crime group ever been brought to light. The ecoterrorists would have covertly killed another "goose" and taken its golden eggs; horse racing would have come one step closer to its demise.

I have come to the conclusion that evil-spirited people *hate-hate-hate* true altruism with a sick passion!!!

Apathy (sloth) is a deadly sin. Neither the Thoroughbred industry nor the government has ever offered to help me fight these evil people who are *exploiting Thoroughbred Racing and the general public.* The biggest problem of all is that there are "dirty hands" on both sides. Greed and deception have control over ecoterrorism –the darkest side of Thoroughbred Racing.

It must have also really infuriated the crime group when they failed in their criminal attempts to extort the SBT horses from Dr. Barr; especially when Dr. Barr donated the top Star Barn horses to the Trust with me as the sole trustee.

Ironically, if the weanlings at Star Barn had been found by the proper authorities to be starved and abused, the weanling manager would have been culpable for their mistreatment.

She of all people should be grateful that all the weanlings that left the farm in Lebanon County were in normal healthy condition. As the paid SBT weanling manager, she was the person solely responsible for the daily care of the weanling at SBT. This willing accomplice has no defense to her despicable role in the terroristic crime scheme. She chose evil over good; she will naturally suffer the consequences!

If anything, the weanlings at SBT were over-fed; most had a deep groove between the muscle and fat on their backs and hips, which was later confirmed by the high body scores they received soon after leaving SBT. How could this be, if terrorists were trying to starve them?

Aided and abetted by the undercover weanling manager, the terrorists parroted "starving SBT weanlings in urgent need of placement". The truth is: SBT never ran out of feed for the horses keep at the farm as being maliciously claimed by the crime group. The weanling manager had been instructed to put feed in the creep feeders for the weanlings and nursing foals twice daily. This was in addition to grass and high-quality hay that were always available. Nursing foals always had access to mother's milk and often ate with their mothers when the mares were fed. Furthermore, the weanling manager was instructed to let Dr. Barr or I know if any of the weanlings were not doing well; which she never did.

In addition to being fed twice daily by the staff, I fed the weanlings and nursing foals a third time after the SBT staff had left the farm; just to make sure that they were well-fed and that the hostile vet would not be able to find anything wrong with them. Furthermore, once it became obvious that we were being stalked and harassed by the terrorists, I also regularly checked the creep feeders during the day. If they were empty, I would fill them with a high-quality "Pelleted Growth Formula".

All the horses that left the farm in Lebanon County left the farm in healthy condition; and, because numerous false reports had reached their new destinations before the horses did, they were all investigated and/or examined upon their arrival in Fredericks County, MD; York County, PA; and, Adams County, PA and were reported to be in good condition by the proper authorities and veterinarians there.

Those that live in glass houses should not throw rocks. While working for SBT, the undercover weanling manager (the terrorists' key witness) was seen putting feed into the truck of her car; she was caught sleeping on the job at least four times; and, she often padded her time sheet with extra hours.

For her major role in the conspiracy, the weanling manager felt entitled to her pick of the extorted horses – she ended up with 3 high-quality Thoroughbreds and wanted more. She and the solicited vet were the most despicable traders of all!

As a licensed veterinarian with over 40 years of practical experience and as the founder and director of Animal Health Safety and Welfare, a 501 (c) 3, non-profit organization, I often provided pro bono veterinary services to animal rescue groups and animal law enforcement groups in Middle Tennessee. As part of my investigations, I used blood tests as absolute proof of whether or not an animal was starved or suffering from an illness. Unlike the vet working undercover for the terrorists, I did not pull blood on obviously healthy horses. Her greed was her downfall and is a prime example of the *ignorance of being evil and unjust.*

Although it was intended to find something wrong with the SBT weanlings (and greed), the blood work done by the undercover vet prior to the horses leaving Lebanon County is absolute proof that the Trust weanlings were healthy and not starved prior to leaving Lebanon County. However, this relevant information was later intentionally withheld from the Court in Adams County, PA.

Post Script - A year later, Dr. Barr tried to collect $20,000 plus in outstanding board and training bills due from a former client; ironically, this exposed her as one of the ecoterrorists who helped put SBT out of business. This was especially egregious on her part, since SBT and I had only done kind things for her and her horses.

The terroristic "feeding frenzy" that occurred as the SBT operation came to an end caused me to scrutinize the past history of SBT. What I thought was really bad employees, bad luck, unusual accidents, and/ or a cursed operation - took on a totally different appearance when the undercover ecoteurs started coming out from their hiding places. Three had even signed statements that they were not aiding and abetting the criminal activities of the group.

How should you evaluate people? The simple answer is: you must judge a tree by its fruit and a person by their deeds. Don't listen to what people say; look at what they actually do; look at the facts and not at created false impressions!

"What happened to Star Barn Thoroughbreds?" was the headline used by one investigative reporter. Since the ecoterrorists had infiltrated and had considerable control over the media, I saw it as another poke at a "dead horse" – or should I say as a poke at several dead and stolen horses. The fact is that the Truth was never printed by the ecoterrorists' controlled media.

I pondered over-and-over in my mind "what just happened?" and "why would a legitimate charitable operation that had nothing but good and charitable things planned - be so egregiously attack (without a hint of justification) by another legitimate non-profit organization. The answer soon became apparent – greed and envy!

I finally came to the conclusion that it was never the ecoterrorists intention to rescue horses; not a single horse was ever rescued from SBT by the crime group; that was just a cover for their sophisticated crime scheme to exploit the Thoroughbred industry. They knew that the Star Barn horses did not need to be rescued; there objectives were to put SBT out of business; to fraudulently solicit donations; and, to take the horses under the tainted color of the law and use the high-quality Thoroughbreds for personal gain.

The quickest way for the terrorists to do this was to "rid the Thoroughbred business of the good Dr. Truitt". This was nothing short of ecoterrorism! A fundamental truth is that there is no shame in being hated by evil people! Evil and ignorant people often envy and hate good, just, and wise people!!

Knowing: that the allegations made to vilify Dr. Barr and me were outrageous and insane lies; that their inhumane treatment of the targeted horses was without a conscience; and, that their unlawful activities were ignored, tolerated, condoned, and/or not enforced by the Justice Systems - I searched for an answer and found that the group's methods of operation fit the textbook profile of psychopaths/terrorists. Star Barn Thoroughbreds and its parent organization Agrarian County had planned to do a lot of good for PA and for the Thoroughbred industry – all despicably sabotaged!

CHAPTER 14

Aggravated Criminal Sabotage

Let's take a closer look at Agricultural Vandalism and Criminal Sabotage. When these crimes are committed against the owners of agriculture related businesses, they are usually aggravated crimes that are intended to harm the owners and to prevent the owner from participating in a particular agriculture business.

PA Codes Title 18 Crimes and Other Offenses - Chapter 33 § 3309 - **Agricultural Vandalism**. (a) Offense defined.--A person commits the offense of agricultural vandalism if he *intentionally or recklessly defaces, marks or otherwise damages the real or tangible personal property of another*, where the property defaced, marked or otherwise damaged is *used in agricultural activity or farming*. (b) Grading.--*Agricultural vandalism is a felony of* the third degree if the *actor intentionally causes pecuniary loss in excess of $5,000....* (c) Definition.--As used in this section, the term "agricultural activity" and "farming" include *public and private research activity*, records, data and data-gathering equipment related to *agricultural products as well as the commercial production of agricultural crops, livestock....*

Theft of tack, tools, feed, supplies, gasoline, etc. became common place at SBT. Destruction of farm vehicles and equipment was common; two dump trucks, a Side Kick, two commercial mowers, and two lawn mowers, etc. were sabotaged. The brakes failed twice on my farm vehicle. The last time, the saboteurs had ripped off *all* the inside door handles so that I could not get out of the vehicle. I feel that this goes beyond vandalism; I feel that the psychopathic in-group would have rejoiced, if I had been killed or seriously injured – much like they did back in 2012 when they thought that, Jockey's Dream, had been killed; and, then again a couple of years later when they allegedly found his headless body.

On another occasion, the exhaust stack on the farm tractor blew up throwing shards of metal back into my face shortly after I had just started mowing a pasture.

On another occasion the bolts underneath the commercial mover were loosened and fell out causing me to lose control of the mower. I was able to crash the mower into a tree to keep it from going over a steep embankment and onto the highway.

[* Note - In my mind these vicious acts, brought up the thought of the sudden and unsolved helicopter crash that killed the two previous owners of the farm. Putting water into the fuel tanks of motorized vehicles and equipment seemed to be a signature act of criminal sabotage used by the terrorists. This certainly could bring down a helicopter shortly after takeoff; and, then go undetected when the helicopter crashes, explodes, and burns.]

*Sabotage is a deliberate action aimed at weakening another entity through subversion, obstruction, disruption, or destruction. In a workplace setting, sabotage is the conscious withdrawal of efficiency generally directed at causing some change in workplace conditions. One who engages in sabotage is a saboteur. *As a rule, saboteurs try to conceal their identities because of the consequences of their actions.*

Criminal sabotage is defined by law as: Whoever, with intent that his or her act shall, or with reason to believe that it may, injure, interfere with, interrupt, supplant, nullify, impair, or obstruct the owner's or operator's management, operation, or control of any agricultural, stock raising, ... or any other **public or private business** or commercial enterprise, wherein **any person is employed for wage**, shall willfully damage or destroy, or attempt or threaten to damage or destroy, any property whatsoever, or shall unlawfully take or retain, or **attempt or threaten unlawfully to take or retain, possession or control of any property** ... used in such business or enterprise, shall be guilty of criminal sabotage.

Because these crimes were intended to facilitate the commission of the greater crimes, (theft by deception, extortion, ecoterrorism, and possibly murder) all would be classified as "aggravated" crimes.

Opening stall doors, barn doors and perimeter gates - all at the same time - was another common act of vandalism that was commonly used by the covert ecoterrorists. Tearing down 16' sections perimeter fence was also often used by the ecoterrorists to let horses out onto major highways; thus, putting the horses and vehicle operators at risk of a catastrophic accident. This also puts farm owners at risk of catastrophic liability.

Giving horses drugs to alter their race performance, or even to kill them, is also used by the ecoterrorists. This puts the trainer at risk of losing his license and/or even being wrongfully convicted of a felony. The undercover ecoterrorists use all kinds of cruel and sophisticated techniques to sabotage a horse's performance, which often puts the horse's life at risk. (Hall of Fame trainer, Bob Baffert, had several horses mysteriously fall dead during or just after training. I highly suspect foul-play in those deaths! *Update after I wrote this book - traces of an anticoagulant, Rodenticide, was later found in the blood of one of Baffert's dead horses and six other dead horses that collapsed and died of hypovolemic shock after working out!!! The traces of poisoning were not high enough to kill the horses; until they exerted themselves while racing or training - causing them the hemorrhage and bleed to death internally!!)

Cases of induced abortions and colics will also skyrocket when ecoterrorists are at work. I also suspect that tampering with trailer hitches while targeted horses are being transported is another vicious act used by undercover ecoterrorists.

I also suspect that undercover ecoterrorists use therapeutic devices such as lacers and shock wave to compromise the performance of horses during their training and racing; and, to cause targeted horses to break down during training and racing. While these medical devices can be used to treat certain types of lameness, they can also be used by undercover ecoterrorists to maliciously harm horses; and, even to cause catastrophic injuries to horses and riders.

Lacers can be used from a distance to harm a horse and to "make them go crazy". Shock wave can be used to cause micro-fractures of the bones which are very painful to the horse and may result in a full-blown fracture during the exertion of racing or training.

CHAPTER 15

Aggravated Animal Cruelty

In a million years, I would have never imagined the ruthless things that happened to the horses at SBT. I have to admit that I was naïve. My experience in Nashville was only an inkling of what hardcore ecoterrorists are capable of doing. While the corrupt government officials in Nashville despicably seized and killed animals masked as a "public service", the domestic terrorists in PA maimed, seized, stole, and killed horses out of pure evil – all for personal gain!

The most deceptive and disturbing thing about Aggravated Animal Cruelty with the intent to commit the crime of *Ecoterrorism* is that the despicable acts are committed by *psychopaths* disguised as "Animal Rights Activists" and "Animal Lovers"!!!!!!!

One integral part of the ecoterrorism crime scheme is the use of undercover employees to vandalize and sabotage the agriculture operation. These saboteurs are often considered by the owners to be their most loyal and trusted employees!!!

PA Title 18 Chapter § 5511: *Cruelty to animals*;

(c) Cruelty to animals.-- (1) A person commits an offense if he wantonly or cruelly ill-treats, overloads, beats, otherwise abuses any animal, or *neglects any animal as to which he has a duty of care, whether belonging to himself or otherwise*, or abandons any animal, or *deprives any animal of necessary sustenance, drink, shelter or veterinary care,* or access to clean and sanitary shelter which will protect the animal against inclement weather and preserve the animal's body heat and keep it dry.

*"**Normal agricultural operation**": Normal activities, practices and procedures that farmers adopt, use or engage in year after year* in the production and preparation for market of poultry, livestock .... As a matter of law, **Thoroughbred horses are livestock used in agriculture activities.**

What I first perceived as insubordination; incompetence; and/or pure laziness (the proverbial "good help is hard to find syndrome) - turned out to be *a nightmare of satanic proportion.* Criminal sabotage, aggravated agriculture vandalism, and aggravated animal cruelty with the intent to commit ecoterrorism were common place at SBT - but *masterfully disguised.* The real sick thing about ecoterrorists is that they insanely want total control of things necessary and dear to their victims; even if, it means depriving the owners of their beloved horses by stealing, maiming, and killing the horses!

I am now certain that at least 3 mares were intentionally and brutally harmed by what now appears to be "signature" gunshot wounds near their private parts; in these three cases the wounds were a little off the mark - close to their vulvas – otherwise I probably would never had figured out what had happened. Looking back, I suspects that the deaths of 3 other mares and 4 or 5 foals may have been caused by similar acts of *merciless animal cruelty.* Except that in those cases there were no visible entry wounds; the projectile must have entered directly into the private parts leaving no visible external signs. Mares treated by other vets and me - and my autopsy on the last killed foal – support my conclusions about this unconscionable signature act of despicable cruelty!

Judging by their silent inactions in these cases, the ecoterrorists obviously intended to hide these despicable acts of cruelty; *the terrorists kept completely silent about these egregious acts of animal cruelty and their undercover "authorities" refused to investigate these despicable acts of animal cruelty.* It is clear that ecoterrorists do not want the public to find out about these most *profound evil acts.* It is obvious that *the ecoterrorists did not want duped accomplices, law enforcement, or the public to know about these unconscionable acts of animal cruelty.*

In their twisted minds, the terrorists covertly killed Star Barn and Trust horses because – in their words - *"you couldn't run a dead horse".* And, of course you can't breed a dead horse.

Only when they think that the targeted owner can be framed for their covert terroristic acts, do the ecoterrorists bring the horrendous acts to the attention of the public - like with the alleged *"multiple deaths"* and/or *"beheading"* of our multiple Grade I winning Thoroughbred stallion, Jockey's Dream!!!

Duped officials and/or willing accomplices quickly and quietly dismissed my allegations that someone had intentionally harmed our horses and that some of the employees were sabotaging SBT. Even though one veterinary practice treated a number of the suspected victims, they ignored my concerns that one of their associates was usurping the medical investigative position at the Lebanon County Humane Society, trespassing on SBT property, and intentionally harassing SBT.

I found out later that the LCHS never actually hired the investigating vet; the same vet that while providing professional services to SBT, intentionally failed to treat two weanlings; maliciously filed complaints against SBT; and, then investigated her own false complaints. Ironically, the ecoterrorists later turned on the undercover vet and the Humane Society officer, for not (falsely) prosecuting Dr. Barr and me. According to the alpha leader, the vet and the officer "didn't do their jobs well".

> [*Note - Ecoterrorists often turn on duped accomplices, after the accomplice has completed their conspiratorial roll; or, if the accomplice was unable to complete their roll to the satisfaction of the alpha leaders! Satirically speaking - Like the Devil – once he deceives his following into doing his evil works; he will use them as fuel for the fires of Hell.]

The psychopaths/ecoterrorists (including paid Star Barn employees who were responsible for the care of the horses) seemed to be insanely angered that they could not frame Dr. Barr or me for animal cruelty. The group openly criticizes the Lebanon County Humane Society for not filing charges.

As soon as the undercover terrorists went public in July of 2011, I was on to them. And I also suspected that SBT had some betrayers working undercover for them. From that point forward, I did my best as a volunteer to make sure that Dr. Barr and SBT was not framed and maliciously prosecuted as happened so often to innocent targeted victims in Nashville! I don't think that Dr. Barr ever knew what hit him!!

All the ecoterrorists had to rely on were their despicable lies about SBT, Dr. Barr, my wife, my business relations and me. It must have been frustrating for the undercover saboteurs and the other coconspirators when I, *while volunteering my services,* kept coming to the rescue of the injured and/or intentionally harmed animals; and, feeding animals that they were intentionally trying to starve. However, that did not stop them from later harming and killing the Trust horses, after they had been taken by deception, leased, and/or fostered out to the Trust's business associates.

One of my favorite foals at Star Barn had her upper lip mutilated! Since horses use their lips to eat, this unconscionable act of cruelty was probably intended to cause the filly to painfully starve to death. Even after I had surgically re-attached the filly's upper lip, the undercover weanling manager intentionally failed to feed the young foal as instructed; I personally went out into the field and privately hand-fed the filly until she had recovered. That filly later died after I had fostered her out; I suspect she had been specifically targeted and killed.

I now highly suspect that another nursing foal was brutally killed, just prior to that. It was made to appear to be a paddock accident!! Earlier the day she died, the beautiful daughter of Jockey's Dream out of Static Discharge left her mother, walked over to where I was working, and wanted to be rubbed. I petted and talked to the filly for several minutes. Sometime during the night she was killed!!

As I said before, if I showed any affection for any of the horses, it was like putting the mark of death on them!!

Another outstanding daughter of Jockey's Dream was tragically killed by undercover terrorists about a year later. She too was one of my favorites. I was crying so hard during her autopsy that I could hardly see. Her rectum had been brutally ruptured!!

CHAPTER 16

Key Facts about the Star Barn Scam

*Even though the **"Star Barn Saga"** (as the terrorists liked to call it) was over on Oct. 28, 2011; the well-camouflaged **"Star Barn Scam"** continued to be a "rich" source of personal gain for members of the crime group. See the June 2014 Article in the Pennsylvania Equestrian Magazine. Members of the crime group were still soliciting donations to care for stolen Trust horses and blaming Star Barn Thoroughbreds for the death of horses that weren't even born when SBT was forced out of business; and, the death of Jockey's Dream who was never owned by Star Barn!!*

A well-orchestrated criminal conspiracy put Star Barn Thoroughbreds out of business; but, their attempts to extort the SBT and Trust horses failed. Therefore, the crime group targeted the Charitable Trust, Star Barn Thoroughbred Breeders' Trust-A.

[*You may have noticed that old people like me often repeat stories about certain events in their lives. Some of us realize it and others don't. So when your grandpa keeps repeating his stories, he wanted you remember them; they were important to him - and may contain some words of wisdom.]

There is also scientific reason for this; and, the reason why terrorists use the devious technique of parroting lies to vilify their targets and to create false impressions. To retain information in long-term memory one must put something in short-term memory approximately six times. The primary reason that I am repeating key facts in this book is to counter the

---

parroted lies of the ecoterrorists, which is their subtle and effective way of brainwashing their targeted audience.

In Nashville, I learned that psychopaths and corrupt government officials will lie on the witness stand and persuade their accomplices to commit perjury to reinforce the same lies. They play by no rules; especially, *"thou shall not bear false witness".*

This devious tactic often fools even the most seasoned judge and will unconscionably discredit an extremely outnumbered victim.

Since psychopaths/terrorists/corrupt government officials are masters of deception; they often use the above technique in their scams. Several members of the crime group will parrot the same outrageous lies. They will repeat lies over and over until others start to perceive them as true. The scientific reason for this is that the subconscious mind cannot tell the difference between reality and fantasy. Repeated affirmations (whether fact or fiction) program the subconscious mind; and, eventually the subconscious mind takes control over the conscious mind; in other words, "garbage in – garbage out".

Even if caught in a lie, psychopaths create confusion by spinning the lie in another direction; they will twist the story yet again to create something that others might believe.

It took me a long time to figure out the crime scheme used by the ecoterrorists; even though, I was probably the main target. Once a psychopath's lies are perceived as the truth; only ultimate reality and absolute truth will vindicate a victim that has been persecuted and vilified.

> *A seasoned psychopathic in-group can get their targeted audience to believe almost anything; no matter how insane their lies may be; lies are the primary tool of their perverted profession. In the words of the corrupt government officials in Nashville - "Perception is all that matters."*

Lying by omission is also an integrity flaw of psychopaths/terrorists/corrupt politicians. This tool of deception was expertly used by the ecoterrorists *after* they had successfully vilified SBT and Dr. Barr and forced SBT out of business. Like with the Ohio Scam, they have kept the Star Barn Scam alive by omitting the fact that *SBT no longer owned a single horse.*

Above all things, knowing the truth and having a conscience are the most important things needed for a person (and a society) to staying in touch with reality. However, to an organized crime group and corrupt government officials *perception is all that matters*; therefore, they will "parrot" outrageous lies about their victims until many perceive the fabrications as the truth.

Another sinister objective of filing false reports and parroting outrageous lies is so that the victim of a psychopathic in-group will be perceived as *the pathological liar;* and, victim's complaints against the group will not be taken seriously by law enforcement. Since the subconscience does not know the difference between reality and fantasy; if lies about the victim are repeated often enough, even those with a conscience start to subconsciously believe the fabrications.

Omitting key facts will also keep duped accomplices and duped law enforcement in the dark. Most of all, psychopaths depend on the ignorance of their duped marks (victims and accomplices).

The following are important Truths about the Star Barn Scam:

When Dr. Barr leased the farm in Grantville, PA in October of 2009, he kept the former employees of Regal Heir and Pennsylvania Thoroughbred Farms, LLC; some were undercover saboteurs already working with the terrorist group. The alpha leader conveniently had undercover people in place at SBT from the beginning with the criminal intent to interfere with my employment with SBT and to exploit SBT. The alpha leader in California claimed that she knew my every move *from the beginning!*

After October 28, 2011, not even the outrageous lies that the crime group had created and continually reinforced about SBT, Dr. Barr and I gave the group any rights or justification for the despicable criminal acts against the Charitable Trust and its innocent beneficiaries.

Once SBT was forced out of existence; it had no horses that the group could target; however, since that time, the scam to exploit SBT has been continuously used to bring in donations – and to deprive the Charitable Trusts and its beneficiaries of all their assets.

In Jan. 2010, Agrarian Country, a 501 (c) 3 non-profit hired me as the general manager of Star Barn Thoroughbreds, the equine division of its proposed International School of Agriculture.

On or around February 1, 2010, with my assistance, the Board of Directors of Agrarian Country established Star Barn Thoroughbred Breeders' Trust – A, an irrevocable Charitable Trust. Dr. Robert Barr and I were appointed as the Trustees.

In the spring of 2010, several quality Thoroughbreds worth millions of dollars were donated to Agrarian Country and the Trust. Subsequently, the horses that belonged to the Trust and its beneficiaries had the potential to generate over $20 million of income for our Charitable Trust.

Individual who contributed assets, capital and/or services to SBTBT-A, became the donors and/or beneficiaries of the Trust. Contrary to the terroristic scam, I did not defraud anyone. Fraud is just another despicable psychopathic trait that terrorists like to project onto their targeted victims.

In reality, the terrorists harmed, stole and killed horses that belong to the very beneficiaries that they claim were defrauded. This is a key fact that the terrorists have kept silent. Furthermore, in addition to all the Trust horses that the terrorists covertly killed, *all the stolen horses that have survived are still legally the property of the Trust.*

As a matter of law, the donors and beneficiaries of the Trust have legal and contractual rights to benefit from (and not to be deprived of) the tangible and intangible property of the Trust; including the horses, the contracts rights, the track earnings and the PA Breeders, Owners and Stallion awards.

Once the ecoterrorists sabotaged SBT out of existence; all the horses that the crime group continued to misrepresent as belonging to SBT; in reality, belonged to the Charitable Trust and its beneficiaries. This was an undisputable legal fact that the ecoterrorists could not *spin* in any direction; therefore, the ecoterrorist were very careful to omit this bit of reality and made sure that this *undisputable* legal facts was withheld.

As the Trustee, I have a legal obligation to manage the tangible and intangible property of the Trust for the enjoyment and benefit to its beneficiaries. I take these legal, moral and ethical duties and obligations seriously; which is something that the morally depraved terrorists are not capable of comprehending.

> *For their scam to continue to work, the crime group had to convince their duped accomplishes, donors, the News Media, and law enforcement that all the targeted horses still belonged to the maliciously vilified SBT and Dr. Barr.*

> *In reality, except for a few of its top horses that it kept and donated to the Trust, Star Barn had sold or given away all of its horses by the time it went out of business on Oct. 28, 2011. As a matter of fact, like Jockey's Dream, most of the Trust horses never belonged to Star Barn Thoroughbreds - at any time.*

I have never been an officer, director, principal or owner of SBT at Agrarian Country or Agrarian Country; I was never more than an extremely hardworking and loyal employee and volunteer. Furthermore, I was laid-off as the general manager of SBT in Nov. of 2010, because the hampered funding for Agrarian Country never materialized.

[*I highly suspected that the terroristic crime group played a role in sabotaging the funding process. I also suspect that if I had not interfered with undercover terrorists' control of SBT at the beginning, the funding would have gone through without a hitch. In fact, the terrorists were probably looking forward to getting their hands on the millions in funding. And, if they were not going to benefit, no one would; especially, Dr. Barr or me.]

[*Note - *It is now obvious that the paid undercover ecoterrorists unconscionably felt no loyalty to Star Barn Thoroughbreds, their employer – or remorse for their despicable acts of aggravated criminal sabotage and animal cruelty.*]

Let us back up a year or so - In retrospect, in Nov. of 2010, I was laid-off as the general manager of SBT @ AC, at which time I was officially relieved of my duties and obligations as the general manager SBT, but not to the Trust, a distinct and separate legal entity. However, the Trust horses were still under the care, custody and control of SBT and its paid employees; including, some of the undercover ecoterrorists.

After I was laid-off as the general manager of SBT in Nov. 2010, full-time paid employees (some undercover saboteurs) were assigned specific management positions and the duties and responsibilities of those positions at SBT. As a matter of law, the full-time paid SBT employees were *culpable* for the care and safety of the Star Barn Thoroughbred horses. This was another fact that the terrorists secretly guarded to insure that it did not reached their duped accomplices, donors, and law enforcement.

The paid undercover ecoteurs were instrumental in sabotaging the SBT breeding and racing operation; and, in creating and spreading the false allegations parroted by the crime group. Ironically, the paid undercover coconspirators were also culpable for the care and safety of the Star Barn and Trust horses; making their allegations against their employer *self-incriminating*.

For the entire year of 2011, I served Agrarian Country and The Barco Group, LLC as a part-time consultant. Barco Group, LLC had made considerable contributions to Agrarian Country and its equine division, Star Barn Thoroughbreds. When it came to my part-time consulting job, I made sure that they got their money's worth by volunteering 80+ additional hours per week.

Even after I had been laid-off by SBT, I was very concerned for the health, safety and welfare of the Trust's horses. So after being laid-off as the general manager, I repeatedly reminded paid managing employees of SBT at AC of their duties and responsibilities. I altruistically volunteered 80+ hours per week to assure that the Trust horses were properly cared for. I continually and voluntarily performed tasks that paid SBT employees failed to do; thus, unknowingly mitigating the damages done by the saboteurs/vandals/terrorists/psychopaths.

[*Note – The alpha leader of the ecoterrorists never cared for any of the horses; she would dupe her accomplices into doing the crimes and taking horses by theft by deception. All she was interested in was the ill-gotten donations.]

If they were needed, I altruistically purchased feed, hay and veterinary supplies out of my own pocket; even after, I was laid-off. In late June of 2011, the well-orchestrated conspiracy, which had sabotaged SBT and my career for a year and a half by using well-disguised methods of sabotage, transformed into a highly aggressive, publicized overt operation with the criminal intent to *"put Star Barn Thoroughbreds at Agrarian County out of business"* and to *"rid the Thoroughbred industry of the good Dr. Truitt"*.

Although it appears that a partially successful covert attempt was made to extort some of the SBT horses in the late fall of 2010 and early winter of 2011 - the first open aggravated criminal attempt to extort the SBT horses was on July 7, 2011.

After weakening SBT and disabling me, the alpha leader and her people (as parts of their signature crime scheme) thoroughly vilified Dr. Barr and me; attempted to maliciously frame us for animal cruelty; and, twice arrogantly attempted to extort all the SBT horses under the perverted pretense of official right.

After maliciously, falsely and publically accusing Dr. Barr and me of sending horses to "killing pens"; after maliciously, falsely and publically accusing Dr. Barr and me of starving and abusing horses; after maliciously and fraudulently getting me barred from training and racing horses at Penn National; after threatening Dr. Barr and me with full investigations by IRS, FBI, OAG, PNGI, Wall Street Journal, The New York Times, numerous horse magazines, etc. – the alpha leader disclosed her true colors by attempting to coerce Dr. Barr into turning all the SBT and Trust horses over to "her people".

By her own admission, the alpha leader of the crime group and "her people" have infiltrated (and have considerable influence and control over) the Thoroughbred industry, especially in PA; law enforcement agencies; other non-profit organizations including the ASPCA, HSUS and PETA;

public horse auctions; News Media; and, the Thoroughbred race tracks owned and operated by Penn National Gaming.

While the ecoterrorists was parroting their insane claims that horses at SBT were starved and abused, numerous visitors and potential buyers visited the farm on several occasions and were always impressed by the appearance of the horses at SBT. Even the undercover snoops for the crime group were impressed by, and envious of, the SBT horses.

The Pennsylvania Office of the Inspector General was also solicited by the ecoterrorists to investigate (harass) me. They sent two seasoned officers to the farm. The Pennsylvania Horse Breeders Association also sent out 3 representatives to inspect the horses (investigate me).

I gave all these officials personal tours of the farm to view the horses. I could not help but notice that they were somewhat irritated at being duped into investigating the *false reports*. Well into their inspections, after seeing how fat most of the horses were, all of these investigators stopped me short of completing their investigations – saying that they had seen enough.

Prior to the targeted Trust horses leaving Lebanon County, numerous blood samples were taken by the undercover vet. The results confirmed that all the animals in question were healthy and that none of the horses were starving as maliciously claimed by the crime group. Dr. Kevin Brophy, another licensed veterinarian, also examined the weanlings (that were maliciously claimed to be starved and abused) and found them to be in normal healthy condition.

After being laid-off in November of 2010, I also continued to voluntarily train horses for SBT and its clients (including one undercover member of the terroristic crime group). I trained several horses until May 15, 2011 at which time SBT suspended its racing operation; it became obvious that the racing operation was being sabotaged and attempts were being made to frame me for doping horses – which would have subjected me to felony charges.

I was informed by the SBT farrier that horses that I was taking to Penn National to train and/or race were being given a tranquilizer, acepromazine, just before leaving the farm to go to the track. The last horse that was entered to race was intentionally brought to the saddling paddock late causing me to be fined $200 by the track Stewards. The other horses entered that day had been intentionally harmed, causing her to go lame.

After SBT was forced to suspend it racing operation, the crime group then falsely claimed that I had sent horses to slaughter and was starving and abusing horses even though I had been laid-off by SBT several months earlier and now had no horses under my care, custody or control.

Even then, Penn National Gaming aided and abetted the crime group by refusing to let me train or race horses at any of their facilities in the future; thus, preventing me from ever racing any of the Trust horses. Penn National Gaming even refused to let me know who posted the sign in the guard station that prevented me from "entering the back stretch until further notice". By barring me from their track, Penn National Gaming reinforced all the insane lies being parroted by the terrorists.

By the time SBT was forced out of business, the crime group had already destroyed the Trust's business relations Starline Films, Penn National Gaming, and Joseph Moriarty. Even after SBT had gone out of business, the coconspirators continued to *stalk and harm* the Trust horses. And, then they methodically interfered with and unlawfully destroyed all the Trust's new business relations.

The malicious and egregious acts of the terrorists effectively doomed the existence of Star Barn Thoroughbreds and caused Agrarian County to loss $155,000,000 in funding. It cost the local, state and federal economy a projected $3 billion and hundreds of jobs.

> *Ecoterrorism well-defined: The ecoterrorists interfered with all my business relations; defamed and vilified me; and, harmed, killed and stole my Trust horses with the criminal intent of preventing me from participating in Thoroughbred breeding and racing.*

> *Over the next three years, law enforcement ignored my complaints against the crime group and allowed them to continue unimpeded until they had successfully committed all their published acts of terrorism and put the Trust out of business.*

Chapter 17

An Insane Sense of Entitlement

[*I am a senior citizen; I turned 67 on October 26, 2014. I have had a mild stroke and open heart surgery. And, I often repeat things that I want others to remember. My mother and father told me their favorite stories over-and-over; I am now glad they did. To store information in your long-term memory, you must process it in your short-term memory at least 6 times. I used this concept as a college instructor and it worked well for my students. Nothing motivated a student better than a high test score and the praise that followed. Therefore, I will often repeat some important facts and principles. Furthermore, *I will praise and honor anyone who takes up the fight against terrorism of any kind!!!!*]

Aberrantly desiring what belongs to others is the primary motivating factor for terrorists. This is as old as Mankind. Greed and envy (an insane sense of entitlement) have forced charity and kindness out of the souls of psychopaths. Terrorists are psychopaths; they have lost touch with Reality; they have gravely dysfunctional and inhumane souls!

Remember the following things about psychopaths/terrorists:

Psychopathic behavior is often masked by superficial charm; psychologists call it "the mask of sanity".

Psychopaths want to control their victims and anything of value to their targets.

Psychopaths look for vulnerable targets; usually, altruistic, kind, honest, naïve and/or trusting people.

Psychopaths have an insane sense of entitlement to things that belong to others.

Lying is as natural as breathing to the psychopaths.

Laws of God, Laws of Nature and Laws of Humanity are "irrelevant" to psychopaths.

Psychopaths do not see others (humans or animals) as having any rights.

Psychopaths do not have a conscience or a sense of guilt.

Psychopaths are master deceivers and manipulators.

Once you have crossed or exposed a psychopath, you can expect continuing and unending retaliation.

Psychopaths are narcissistic; they play by their own rules.

In their twisted minds, basic rules of humanity such as the following biblical rules do not apply to them:

"Thou shall not kill."

"Thou shall not lie, deceive or bear false witness."

"Thou shall not steal."

"Thou shall not covet thy neighbor's property."

"Do not pass along untrue reports."

"Do not cooperate with an evil man by affirming something you know is false."

"Do not join mobs intent on evil."

"A man's property is no excuse for twisting justice against him."

"Keep far away from falsely charging anyone; never let an innocent person be falsely prosecuted."

"You must not exploit widows and children".

"If a man steals an animal then kills or sells it, he shall pay restitution of five to one."

Terrorists must stay up at night trying to find ways to get away with breaking the rules of humanity; terrorists are obsessed in finding ways to destroy their victims and take the things that the victims value most. The alpha leader of one terroristic in-group often brags that she "works" 17 hours a day. It must take her at least that long to keep her fabricated stories straight and to find new ways to harm her targeted victims!

Greed and envy are insane desires to deprive others of their property; property that you have no need for; or interest in. Terrorists have an insane sense of entitlement to whatever belongs to their targeted victims. This insane behavior trait became even more obvious after the ecoterrorists forced SBT out of business. The "Star Barn Saga" (as the ecoterrorists like to call it) was over and done with on Oct. 28, 2011; all the damage and destruction that could have possibly been done to Agrarian Country, SBT and Dr. Barr was accomplished. Out of greed and envy, the ecoterrorists had maliciously deprived Agrarian County of its property and its dreams - all the good things that Agrarian County had planned for the citizens of Pennsylvania and the World.

However, *out of pure evil*, the ecoterrorism continued as the crime group insanely and methodically depriving our Charitable Trust of all its property and all the benefits that the property would have brought to the innocent beneficiaries of the Trust; including, Collin's Classic for Kids with Cancer; The Make-A-Wish Foundation; and, St. Jude Children's Research Hospital.

After egregiously sabotaging Star Barn from its beginning to end, the ecoterrorists still had an *insane obsession* to prevent the donors and beneficiaries of the Trust from benefiting from their contract rights, horses and the PA breeders awards.

The evil in-group had a depraved obsession to deprive the Charitable Trust of all its tangible and intangible property; albeit by death or taking illegal possession of its horses. They had a malicious desire to prevent the Trust horses from racing any of its horses. In the words of the ecoterrorists – *"good* news for you Paul E. Truitt; none of these horses will ever race"; "they are all going to die"; and, "you couldn't run a dead horse".

Even though it was common knowledge that SBT no longer owned a single horse, *the insane group went to great lengths to create the false impression that all the Charitable Trust's horses belonged to the thoroughly defamed SBT and Dr. Barr. Duped accomplices and the News Media went along with the terrorists and continually reinforced the false impression; although, they knew the truth.*

Why did the ecoterrorists want to make their duped accomplices, benefactors, and law enforcement believe that the horses belonged to SBT? The answer is simply - there was no way for this depraved group to justify *"maliciously taking and wrongfully disposing of"* the property belonging to the donors and designated beneficiaries of a Charitable Trust; especially, since some of them were widows and "terminally ill children". *There is absolutely no way to "twist" the laws or the facts in a way that they could legally make it appear that they were justified in depriving the Trust and its beneficiaries of their property – absolutely none!!!!*

[*As a matter of fact, all the Trust horses that were taken by theft by deception, coercion or extortion; still legally belong to the Trust; and, possessing the stolen horses or selling the stolen horses is a felony. Law enforcement and the News Media were made aware of this, yet they did absolutely nothing!]

Terrorists have no justification for their despicable acts; so *they must create and reinforce a "fictitious" world that justifies their insanity.* They first ambush and harm their victims from undercover. Then they must fabricate lies and reinforce those lies to dupe their accomplices and the general public.

> [*I guess the things that I have noticed most about terrorists – is that they often vilify their targets by projecting their own despicable traits onto the victims. Psychopaths and terrorists are often what they maliciously portray their targeted victims to be. For instance, they portrayed me to be a pathological liar; a sick SOB; a sick POS; a fraud; someone who abuses animals; someone that should not still be walking; someone who should be hung; someone who should be in jail; an evil person who should rot in Hell, etc.]*

> *While anger, envy and greed are deadly sins that control most terrorists; pride and cowardice will destroy their duped accomplices. They are too proud to admit that they have been duped; and, to cowardly to come to the aid of their maliciously harmed victims. Pride of course is an express ticket to Hell - go straight past Paradise;*

follow the devil into Hell; and, then take a high dive into the biblical "Lake of Fire".

Without any justification or provocation, the alpha leader and "her people" targeted and sabotaged Star Barn Thoroughbreds from its beginning in Oct. of 2009 until its demise in Oct. of 2011. I believed that Star Barn Thoroughbreds (like its predecessors, Regal Heir Farm and Pennsylvania Thoroughbred Farms, LLC) was targeted simply because they were a high profile Thoroughbred breeding and racing operation with lot of assets to exploit!

[* Note – Just a word about the undercover employees who chose evil over good - many simply wasted their talents!! In the past, I mentored employees with similar talent who become leading jockeys and trainers. At times, I was managing some incredible talent in PA; yet, they chose to turn criminal and self-destruct by aiding and abetting the ecoterrorists.]

"Those who recognize and stand up to psychopaths can expect unending retaliation." – R. Hare

Psychopathic terrorists have an obsession for controlling their victims. Even after being found out, they will continue to seek ways to *covertly* harm their victims. Terrorists follow no rules or laws of humanity; in their own words, court orders are "irrelevant".

A man of my education, experience, character, and a background of working with legitimate non-profit organizations and animal related law enforcement would certainly posed a threat to perverted non-profit organizations such as those operated by the Mid-Atlantic ecoterrorists; therefore, I can't help but feel that I was a primary target all along; I threatened their control over the existing Thoroughbred operation; and after they sabotaged SBT, I took control of both the targeted SBT and Trust horses; *horses that they insanely felt entitled to!*

The evil in-group tried to disable me from the day I moved to PA. And they have not stopped since!!!!!

Dr. Barr and I did not realize what an integral part the most trusted undercover SBT employees and a couple of clients had played in the signature crime scheme; not until SBT had been forced out of business and the undercover saboteurs and clients went public and continued to aid and abet the criminal activities of the terrorists. It did not become clear until a year after SBT had gone out of business; when on Oct. of 2012, Dr.

Barr sent me his notes from a recorded phone conversation that he had on July 7, 2011 with the alpha leader of crime group.

Looking back – a covert attempt was made to take the Star Barn horse under the color of the law in late 2010/early 2011, shortly after I had been laid-off. A second open attempt to extort the SBT horses was in July of 2011; and, a third veiled, but highly coercive, attempt was made by the group's undercover vet who was supposed to be treating a couple of the SBT weanlings at the time. This happened just before SBT went out of business.

The psychopathic terrorists had an insane sense of entitlement to the SBT horses. Forcing SBT out of business was not enough to satisfy them, they still wanted the SBT horses; so they insanely targeted all the horses that belonged to the Charitable Trust.

Neither Dr. Barr nor I knew that we had been targeted and that SBT had been sabotaged for the entire first year and 9 months of operation – or that we were going to be under siege as long as necessary *"to put SBT out of business"* and *"to rid the Thoroughbred industry of the good Dr. Truitt"*.

Terrorism is mostly twisted politically and religious beliefs; politics and religion gone insane!!! The ecoterrorists had an insane desire to deprive SBT and the Trust of their horses; all they needed to insanely justify stealing and killing the horses was to vilify SBT, Dr. Barr and me; and, to dupe the public and law enforcement into believing that they had an official right to "rescue" the horses.

It became brutally apparent later that the terrorists did not want to share their "spoils" with any outsiders; especially, the helpless beneficiaries of the Trust. In their twisted minds, the donors and beneficiaries of the Trust had done nothing to "deserve" any benefits from the horses, the contract right, or breeder's awards; that was all Dr. Truitt's doings; and, he is our target!!!

> *[Satirically speaking for the insane ecoterrorists, "We are entitled to the Star Barn horses! After all, we have spent a lot of time and effort into vilifying Dr. Barr and Dr. Truitt. Our undercover people have put a lot of time and effort into sabotaging Star Barn. We have spent a lot of time filing false reports from all over the country. And our undercover people tried their best to starve and abuse the horses at Star Barn and to frame Dr. Barr. We put SBT out of business as we said we would; therefore, we forbid anyone else to benefit from any of "our" horses! And if we can't have the horses, they are all going to die. After all, you couldn't run dead horses. Good news for you Paul E. Truitt, not a one of these horses will ever run or make you money."]*

CHAPTER 18

The Dark Side of the Human Spirit

Our society (and the world) needs to wake up; *all is not fair in love and war – or politics or religion!!!!! Only God is The Perfect Form of Goodness!!!! Most human beings have a Spirit of Good within their souls; which guides and directs them to do what is right; but sadly, there are too many human souls that possess the Spirit of Evil; which inspires them to do evil things.*

> *Fighting terrorism is sometimes like fighting demonic ghosts. Most of the time, they work undercover and are masked by deception. They only come out of the dark shadows when they feel that their victims are disabled and can't fight back.*

The most emotional damage done by ecoterrorists is usually caused by *betrayal* at the hands of undercover terrorists posing as trusted employees, friends, clients, government officials, track officials, media personnel, legal advocates, or business affiliates.

In promoting their perverted cause, anti-Thoroughbred racing activists like to reference to the *dark side* of racing; when in fact *ecoterrorism is the darkest side of Thoroughbred racing; terrorism is the darkest side of humanity!!!!!*

CHAPTER 19

Charitable Trust Despicably Targeted

What happened after Star Barn Thoroughbreds at Agrarian County was forced out of business is even more insane - and despicable! The terrorists maliciously deprived the innocent beneficiaries of our Charitable Trust of their tangible and intangible property with the criminal intent to prevent us from profiting from the lawful activities of Thoroughbred racing and breeding. Ecoterrorism at its most evil!!!

On February 1st of 2010, Agrarian Country created a Charitable Trust (Star Barn Thoroughbred Breeders' Trust-A). Millions of dollars' worth of high-quality Thoroughbreds, capital, and services were donated to the Trust. The altruistic purpose of the Trust was: to help financially troubled Thoroughbred owners; to provide high-quality Thoroughbred horses for Agrarian Country's breeding, racing, education, and research programs; and, to benefit the donors and their designated beneficiaries - including Collin's Classic for Kids with Cancer, St. Jude Children's Research Hospital, and The Make-A-Wish Foundation.

Dr. Barr and I were appointed as the Trustees. When SBT was forced out of business on October 28, 2011, Dr. Barr resigned his position. This left me as the sole trustee.

By that time, the ecoterrorist had already maliciously sabotaged the Charitable Trust's four most important business relations (Star Barn Thoroughbreds at Agrarian County, Penn National Gaming, Starline Films, and Joseph Moriarty). However, I still had a legal and moral obligation to the donors and designated beneficiaries.

Except for the 2010 foal crop, I successfully placed all the Trust's broodmares and 2011-weanlings, including the top horses that had been donated by SBT, by reaching lease/purchase agreements with various farm owners and trainers. This looked like a blessing from God! However, we all know how well God and the Devil get alone!

I can remember how blessed I felt. I would soon be turning 65 and going on social security. I loved working with horses; it seemed more like playing a sport than work. I was planning to retire and just manage the Trust for the benefit and enjoyment of its many beneficiaries.

Pursuant to mutually beneficial agreements – Uriah St Lewis of Bensalem, PA leased 4 horses in training; Franklin Brinkley of OH leased a horse in training; Rebecca Demczyk of OH leased 2 horses in training; Art House of Maine fostered 3 2011-weanlings; Joe Laslo leased 2 open mares and 6 pregnant mares; Randy Rineer adopted 2 open mares and fostered 2 2011-foals; Darlene Townsend adopted 2 fillies just off the track and leased 1 pregnant mare; James Houseman leased 17 2011-weanlings, 2 open mares, 16 pregnant mares, and 1 stallion; Denise McHenry took 1 pregnant mare; and, Paul High adopted 4 2011-weanlings. Several horses from the 2010 crop were also leased out to various owners and trainers. I sold and leased some of the 2010 foal crop, in 2012. Then in the summer of 2013, Jack Frost, a trainer from Arkansas, took the last 10 Trust horses; all from the 2010 foal crop.

These business relations put the Trust in a stable and potentially lucrative economic position. Collectively these agreements would have potentially brought in millions in *benefits* for the Charitable Trust - at little or no expense to the Trust. It would have also potentially benefited all the Trust's business relations.

However, like the corrupt government officials in Nashville, the terrorists were *insanely obsessed* with my every move! Their despicable criminal activities had just started.

As with the beneficial Trust agreements with Agrarian County, Penn National Gaming, Starline Films, and Joseph Moriarty, all the above agreements have since been maliciously interfered with and destroyed by terrorists; the terroristic crime group was *insanely obsessed* with depriving the beneficiaries of the Trust and me of all the horses and potential benefits.

Their well-published goal was to make sure that the good Dr. Truitt does not make any money off any of the horses!!!

At first, I had kept the entire 2010 foal crop and planned to train and race them. However, *the terrorists were not about to let any of the Trust horses escape their wrath!!* Even after I moved the last horses to Paris, KY in the summer of 2013, the terrorists were still intent on putting us completely out of business. I entered into an agreement with Jack Frost to take our last 10 horses-in-training; all from the 2010 foal crop. In less than a year, all those horses had been killed - or harmed to the point that none of them were suitable for racing.

It took the terroristic crime group two years to completely destroy Star Barn Thoroughbreds; it took them another 3 years to deprive the beneficiaries of the Trust of their assets and to put the Charitable Trust out of business. Without any help from law enforcement, the Justice System, the News Media, or any private attorney willing to file a civil complaint against any of the terrorists, the Trust had no horses to fight for!!!

That is - I have given up the *overt* fight. I did consider one retired attorney's advice to finish the game by playing by their rules!!!! However, due to my character, all that I can do is to counter their insane lies with the Truth and Facts of Law.

From this point forward I will leave it up to a higher power to punish the terrorists!!! However, if any of the readers are interested in giving God a hand, let me know. God expects those on His team to fight His battles against Evil while we and the terrorists, psychopaths, tyrants, and corrupt public servants are still here on Earth. After that, God will take care of their souls by placing them on the burn pile!!!!!

I will continue to send out "Requests for Correction, Retraction, and Renunciation to the members of the terrorist group that I feel may have been duped.

I am even offering a REWARD – a conditional reward that is potentially worth as much as $16 million or more! There is no honor among terrorists and sooner or later they will turn on each other!! It is just a matter of time; and, who turns on their coconspirators first!! Evil is naturally self-destructive!

Many members of the crime group have publically self-incriminated themselves; therefore, it is just a matter of time until they are brought to justice! The actual damages are clear; and, it is public knowledge that the following laws have been broken!!!

Back to the Facts of Law:

Pursuant to PA Title 18 Chapter 33 § 3311: *Ecoterrorism* – a person is guilty of ecoterrorism if the person commits a specified offense against *property* intending to do any of the following: (1) *Intimidate or coerce* an individual *lawfully*: (i) *participating in an activity involving animals* ... (2) *Prevent or obstruct* an individual from *lawfully*: (i) *participating in an activity involving animals* ...

A lawful activity involving the use of animals, including any of the following: (5) *Entertainment and recreation.* (6) *Research, teaching* ... (8)

Agricultural activity and farming as defined in section 3309 (relating to agricultural vandalism).

Pursuant to PA Title 18 Chapter 33 § 3309: *Agricultural vandalism.* (c) Definition.--As used in this section, the terms "agricultural activity" and "farming" include *public and private research activity, ... the commercial production of* agricultural crops, *livestock* or livestock products...

Pursuant to PA Title 18 Chapter 39 § 3901: Definitions. *"Property" Anything of value, including real estate, tangible and intangible personal property, contract rights, choses-in-action and other interests in or claims to ... domestic animals....*

Pursuant to agriculture vandalism and ecoterrorism statutes, the *specified offenses* include *damage to tangible or intangible personal property, contract rights, choices in action and other interest in or claim to domestic animals.*

PA Title 18 Chapter 9 § 911: *Corrupt organizations* - The *Attorney General shall have the power and duty to enforce* the provisions of this section, including the authority to issue civil investigative demands pursuant to subsection (f), institute proceedings under subsection (d), and to take such actions as may be necessary to ascertain and investigate alleged violations of this section.

CHAPTER 20

Despicable Acts against Our Charitable Trust

It was common knowledge among the ecoterrorists that Star Barn Thoroughbreds no long owned or had any horses under its care custody or control after Oct. 28, 2011; "The Star Barn Saga" was over!!! However, at this point the crime group was *self-assured* that law enforcement was not going to take any action against them not matter how insane and despicable they acted!! They had succeeded in thoroughly vilifying SBT, Dr. Barr and me; they were sure that their lies were perceived as true and that "no one will take Dr. Truitt seriously from now on"!!

Any group with any sense of decency would have left our Charitable Trust alone. However, many members of the insane crime group had lost touch with reality! What happen from this point in time was even more despicable - pure evil!!!

[*Legal Fact - *There was absolutely no reason or justification for the ecoterrorists to attack the Charitable Trust or to deprive its helpless beneficiaries of their tangible and intangible property.*]

Terrorists (domestic or foreign) are evil people with evil motives; often masquerading as activists with noble political or religious causes. In reality, their primary objective was personal gain; and, they seem to get some kind of perverted pleasure from harming others. In reality, the fight against terrorism (domestic or foreign) is not really a fight between people with different religious beliefs or political views; it is simply a fight between Good and Evil. My hope is that come Judgment Day our souls are going to be judged by our deeds; the fruit that our "spirits" produce; not by our religious or political beliefs or phenotype.

It is no mystery why terrorism is so successful; it is simply because terrorists play by no rules; have no moral values; and, have no conscience or sense of guilt or remorse! Depriving their victims of their lives, freedom, and/or property brings the terrorist a depraved sense of accomplishment and pleasure.

One might ask how ecoterrorists, posing as animal rights activists, can love animal so much; while hating other human beings so much!! In reality, terrorists (domestic or foreign) do not have the capacity to love people or animals; people and animals are merely objects used by terrorists for personal gain and sadistic pleasure.

After SBT (the Charitable Trust's primary donor and business relation) was forced out of business (and had transferred its few remaining Thoroughbreds to the Trust), I felt an even stronger duty and obligation to the beneficiaries of Star Barn Thoroughbred Breeders' Trust – A.

My legal duties and obligations kept me in the fight against these evil beings!!! That and the Spirit of God in my soul – that continuously guides and directs me! Although the terrorists have taken most everything of value from me; they can never deprive me of my spirit! Good spirits are immortal; while the evil in a bad spirit will destroy it!

[*Note – In one of his movies, Denzel Washington's character possibly had the only effective way of dealing with terrorists that harm helpless animals and children. "Arrange a meeting between them and God!!"]

In an effort to rescue the top SBT and SBTBT-A horses for the benefit of those who contributed horses, capital, and services to the Star Barn Thoroughbred Breeders' Trust – A, I had reached agreements with various individuals on behalf of the Trust and its beneficiaries. These agreements placed SBTBT-A in a secure and potentially lucrative economic position. Things looked exceptional good!

After SBT was forced out of business, the twisted and criminal activities of the crime group only intensified!!! This supports the fact that domestic and foreign terrorists play by no rules; have no sense of decency; and, have no conscience!!!

True to their psychopathic character, the ecoterrorists maliciously sought out and systematically destroyed *"all"* the Trust's business relations. Even more despicable, they killed and stole the very horses that would have benefited the donors and beneficiaries; the same donors and their designated beneficiaries that the psychopathic in-group insanely claimed had been defrauded! Furthermore, they despicably took property and benefits from three children's charities that help critically ill children! How evil is that?

Any person doing business with the Trust was ruthlessly and insanely targeted by the crime group. Driven by their insane sense of entitlement to the Trust horses, the ecoterrorists stalked and intentionally destroyed all the Trust's business relations; and then took, harmed, and/or killed many of the Trust's horses; thus, egregiously causing over $20 million in actual damages to the beneficiaries of our Charitable Trust. The collateral damages were several times that amount.

"Got news for you Paul E. Truitt. Not one of the babies will EVER be raced." – A statement made by Deb Jones in early 2012 soon after she and her undercover terrorists had put SBT out of business.

"You couldn't run a dead horse." – Deb Jones in 2014

If justice is done, the despicable lies and threats - so arrogantly published by the terrorists - will surely come back to haunt each and every one of them. *The crime group has insanely carried out their published evil terroristic threats; while law enforcement and the Justice System have ignored their despicable crimes and did nothing.*

What is even more disturbing is that the crime group's duped accomplices and benefactors are too afraid to come forward to help the beneficiaries of the Charitable Trust. How wrong and cowardly is this?

The crime group's *evil obsession* to destroy me; their insane beliefs about who will benefit from the Trust's horses; and, their determination to stalk and interfere with all my economic relations may explain why most of the Trust's broodmares, Jockey's Dream, 2011 Trust foals, and the all the 2012, 2013 and 2014 foals are all dead or missing; Trust horses that have older siblings who have won millions at the track have been insanely taken and maliciously prevented from racing.

The Ultimate Reality is that Trust horses were despicably stolen and killed by the ecoterrorists to insanely keep the helpless beneficiaries of the Charitable Trust from making any money off them; and, to despicably create "shock value" which is being used to fraudulently solicit more donations. The clear well-published intent was to make sure I (their fabricated villain) never made any money off them and to prevent me (their fabricated villain) from participating in Thoroughbred racing; it did not matter to the ecoterrorists who was being harmed, albeit our beloved horses or critically ill children. Like with most acts of terrorism, innocent victims are unconscionably harmed, killed, and maimed!!!

True to their psychopathic character, the terrorists continually invaded my privacy; and, continuously stalked the Trust horses, my business relations, and me. Sometimes going so far as posing as potential buyers; stalking the farms and trainers where Trust horses were kept; coming into my home; and, hacking into my computers.

Posing as legitimate business relations, some uncover ecoterrorists leased horses from the Trust with no intention to pay the Trust its portions of the income from the horses - or to return the horses - classic cases of aggravated theft by deceptions with the criminal intent to commit ecoterrorism. Evil destroys itself!! Justifiably some of the terrorists have been ruthlessly attacked by the group!!

[*Update – As of October 16, 2014, the Trust has been deprived of all the 2010 foals that I guarded as long as I was able.

CHAPTER 21

Turning Lies into Despicable Crimes

Terrorists/psychopaths are able to get away with their despicable crimes because they are master liars and deceivers!!

After the ecoterrorists had forced Star Barn Thoroughbreds out of business, the most despicable thing about them was that they unconscionably stole, harmed, and killed Trust horses; and, the innocent beneficiaries of a Charitable Trust were maliciously deprived of their tangible and intangible property - horses, contract right, PHBA awards, track earnings, and Thoroughbred sales.

The hardcore ecoterrorists and their accomplices have: caused millions in damages to the innocent beneficiaries of the Trust; are responsible for the death of many of the Trust's Thoroughbreds; and, the crime group has maliciously ruined the lives of countless victims – and they have viciously turned-on some of their accomplices!!!

Despicable crimes were facilitated by expertly parroted lies!

Contrary to all the despicable lies parroted by members of the crime group, the Truth is that:

1. My license to practice veterinary medicine in TN has never been revoked.
2. I have never been convicted of animal abuse.
3. The crime group had undercover terrorists working for SBT from the beginning – Oct. 2009 – before I started to work there.

4. I was employed by Star Barn Thoroughbreds as its general manager from Jan. 1, 2010 until Nov. 26, 2010.

5. I have never starved or abused horses.

6. I did not send any horses to slaughter.

7. My wife never sent to slaughter, starved, or abused any horse. She has never owned a single horse!

8. Starline Equestrian Center never sent to slaughter, starved, or abused any horse. SEC has never owned a single horse!

9. Starline Films has never sent to slaughter, starved, or abused any horse. Starline Films has never owned a single horse!

10. Star Barn Thoroughbreds has never sent to slaughter, starved, or abused any horse.

11. After I was laid-off by SBT, undercover members of the group did harmed and killed horses to sabotage Star Barn.

12. The terrorists stalked, took by theft, harmed, and killed several Trust horses, after they forced SBT out of business in Oct. of 2011.

13. Only undercover members of the crime group would know who harmed and killed the horses at SBT; and, the Trust horses after the horses had left SBT.

14. I have never been an officer, owner, or principle of SBT or a partner of Dr. Barr; only a hardworking and loyal employee; and, a volunteer for the last year of its operation.

15. James Houseman III had conspiratorial relationships with alpha leaders Deb Jones and Deb Rogers. After Houseman had taken several Trust horses by theft by deception, he was not able to frame the "The Star Barn Guys" for animal cruelty as planned; therefore, Jones and Rogers turned on him.

16. After Oct. 28, 2011, all the stolen horses that the terrorists want their duped accomplices, donors, and benefactors to believe were still owned by SBT - were, and still are, the legal property of Charitable Trust and its beneficiaries.

17. By creating the false impression that the Trust horses belonged to the thoroughly vilified SBT, the terrorists were able to take the Trust horses under that perverted pretenses; as if they had an official right to do so.

18. The Adams County SPCA wrongfully seized and improperly disposed of 8 healthy Trust foals of 2011.

19. To frame and wrongfully prosecuted "The Star Barn Guys" (Dr. Barr and Dr. Truitt), the Adams County SPCA and/or their coconspirators substituted 9 sick and/or starved weanlings of 2011 for 9 healthy Trust weanlings.

20. Those 9 healthy Trust weanlings were taken by theft by deception and improperly disposed of. They were never seized by or the custody of the Adams County SPCA.

21. With the intent to frame Dr. Barr and/or me, the terrorists created and continually reinforced the false impression that 14 ringers (dead, sick, and/or starved horses) had just arrived in Adams County and belonged to "The Star Barn Guys".

22. In reality, all these ringers had been in the care, custody, and control of the terrorists/coconspirators. The ringers had never been at SBT in Lebanon County; nor had they even been owned by SBT or the Trust.

23. With the help of their undercover ecoterrorists, the Adams Country SPCA wrongfully extorted 17 foals of 2011 from the Trust; including, 2 of my favorite weanlings that had died (after being wrongfully seized and ordered by the court to be returned) and 9 that had never been seized or in the possession of the Adams County SPCA.

24. The corrupt Adams County Justice System threatened me with 17 counts of animal cruelty and $90,000 in restitutions if I did not sign all 17 healthy horses over to the Adams County SPCA.

25. The Adam County SPCA (and later coconspirator James Houseman III) attempted to extort the documentation necessary to register all of 17 Trust foals of 2011; including, the 2 dead Trust horses and the 9 Trust horses that had never been seized or in the possession of the ACSPCA.

26. The ecoterrorists insanely stole, harmed, and killed Trust horses and insanely interfered with *all* the Trust business relations with the criminal intent to prevent "the good Dr. Truitt" from participating the Thoroughbred breeding and racing. [Ecoterrorism]

27. The ulterior motive for harming and killing the Trust horses was to create "shock value" needed by the alpha leaders to fraudulently solicit donations. Their accomplices took stolen horses as secret rewards – their share of the spoils!!!

CHAPTER 22

Terrorists are Master Liars and Manipulators

Terrorists are usually well-prepared by months of planning and ground work. Terrorists are highly effective, because they can create turmoil and confusions in an instance. Once "the bomb goes off" their victims are totally caught totally off-guard by the surprise attack and put on the defensive!!!

Since Dr. Barr was not coerced into giving all the SBT horses to the alpha leader and "her people" in July of 2011, the crime group under the perverted guise of rescuing starved and abused horses created the false impression that SBT, Dr, Barr, my wife, and/or I had sent them to slaughter and that the horses were starved and abused. The ecoterrorists immediately published entire lists of the STB horses, including the Trust horses; and posted - "Sent to slaughter on 7/29/2011".

Aware that the listed horses had a combined estimated value and earning potential in the millions, the ecoterrorists created the false impressive that they had rescued the "starved" and "abused" horses from "slaughter", and that the horses were free for the taking and/or that they were being returned to their previous owners. The ecoterrorists also maliciously claimed that Dr. Barr and I had defrauded the previous owners of the horses. It is now obvious that the whole attack on SBT had been well-organized and the social network had been in place!

It is clear that the malicious intent of the ecoterrorists' Facebook page was to vilify Dr. Barr and me and to facilitate the wrongful taking of the SBT horses. Since the group *never* adopted or rescued a single horse from SBT, it became obvious that the crime group used the Facebook site mostly for the purpose of fraudulently soliciting donations – donations that they claimed were "urgently needed" to care for horses that the group *misrepresented* as rescued from slaughter, abuse, and/or starvation; *horses that in reality had never left SBT.*

Throughout the summer and fall of 2011, Star Barn Thoroughbreds (Dr. Robert Barr, president) and I were defamed, harassed, coerced, and vilified by the terrorists. Furthermore, terrorists from all over the country continually filed false reports of animal cruelty which resulted in numerous unwarranted and harassing investigations by the Lebanon County Humane Society that caused both Dr. Barr and me extreme economic, emotional and physical distress.

Dr. Barr was distressed into having a stroke; my emotional distress precipitated a minor stroke which caused me to lose sight in my left eye. I also had a number of heart attacks which lead to open heart surgery. (*In retrospect, I find it strange that both Dr. Barr lost vision in one of our eyes and the blindness was attributed to mild strokes. Furthermore, several of our horses had problems with just one of their eyes with no apparent injuries. I now suspect something more sinister may have been going on and that it may have involved the undetected use of a lacer from a distance. Terrorism has a way of making the victim paranoid.)

Without any justification, the crime group and its undercover paid SBT saboteurs sabotaged and vandalized SBT from its beginning in Oct. of 2009 until its demise in Oct. of 2011; two whole years of TERROR!!! The yearling manager, broodmare manager, and weanling manager all denied being a part of the conspiracy. Nonetheless, they were required to sign statements warning them of the penalty for participating in the criminal conspiracy to put SBT out of business. Due to my trusting and altruistic nature, I was an easy mark for the young saboteurs. Signing the statements denying their involvement in the crimes only bought the undercover ecoteurs more time. The most trusted employees turned out to be the most deceptive and manipulative. While I was trying to mentor them, the young paid saboteurs continued to deceive me and betray their employer – and me. It was not until these last saboteurs were terminated as employees of SBT and came out from under their cover, did I realize that I had been "duped" by the youngest and most trusted SBT employees. I had also been thoroughly manipulated by a trusted client.

CHAPTER 23

How to Fight Terrorism

I greatly appreciate and admire all the courageous and honorable people who serve God and their country for the good of all Mankind!!

I know that decapitating or shooting one of my beloved horses is not the same as someone's son or daughter getting shot in their classroom; or, a gallant soldier beheaded by psychopathic terrorists; but, I do know that it is time for all good people of the world to take a stand against terrorism of all kinds! We need to have zero tolerance to terroristic acts of any kind. Terrorism is the most heinous disease ever known to Mankind! It is pure evil!

To fight evil you must first recognize and expose it; to fight terrorisms of any kind:

1. *You need to recognize terrorists and their well-disguised crime schemes!*
2. *Then you must expose terrorists to the "Light of Truth"!!*
3. *Law Enforcement and the Justice System must investigate and prosecute terrorism and corruption of all kinds!!!*

   If law enforcement ignores terrorism and corruption and fails to guard good and just citizens against it, then our country and the World has a real problem!

   The thing that I fear most is that this great country of ours is rapidly reaching a point of no return; that the apathy of its good citizens will continue to let psychopaths, terrorists, and, corrupt government officials exploit our country!!! The criminal motives of terrorists (once they have been exposed) are so transparent!! There is no noble political or religious cause; terroristic acts are carried out simply for personal gain and sadistic pleasure.

We are in a fight between Good and Evil!! A fight that all good people of the world must courageously and honorably fight!!

Many good and just citizens of the world are suffering from "naïve prey syndrome"; they fail to recognized social predators and terrorists of any kinds - until the proverbial bomb goes off! Law enforcement and the Justice System then often suffer from ignorance and apathy!! Terrorists insanely believe that a perverted political and/or religious cause give them the right and justification to deprive their targeted victims of their livelihood; interfere with their business relations; to destroy or take their property; and, to deprive their victims of their hopes and dreams – and even their lives. The entire world has to reject the notion that terrorists are merely religious or political activists; when in reality, they are nothing more that psychopathic criminals who must forfeit their human rights for insanely infringing on the rights of other!

Terrorists, psychopaths, tyrants, corrupt government officials – whatever you want to call them – like to operate under the cover of deceit; they are master liar and deceivers; so once they are recognized and exposed to the truth, they are greatly disabled!! This is where Law Enforcement and the Justice System could and should take up the fight! For the sake of all humanity, they must take up the fight!! Terrorists of any kind should be hunted down like the delirious rabid dogs that they are - and disposed of!!!!

Ecoterrorists are capable of most any despicable act that will harm the targeted animals and put the targeted owners out of business. Covertly killing targeted horses is used by ecoterrorists to create shock value!!!! The alleged decapitation of the "stolen" multiple Grade I winner Jockey's Dream was despicably used by the terrorists to raise donations!!! [See June 2014 issue of *Pennsylvania Equestrian*]

Domestic and foreign terrorists are psychopaths; so it is important to *first learn how to recognized psychopathic behavior*; learn how they operate. Once exposed terrorists are not as big a threat. Fight fire with fire. Once you have recognized a domestic terrorist fight back. Get the word around. Speak out. Let everyone know who they are; tell family, friends, business associates, the new media, law enforcement, the whole community. This will help keep you and your loved ones a little safer. At the very least, law enforcement will know who to look for if something happens to you or a loved one!!

One more precaution to targets of terrorism: these crime groups will often stage hostile relations between undercover members of the terrorist group. This totally caught me off guard of few times. This allows unsuspected members of the group to gain your trust and confidence. Remember that terrorists work in packs and that they are master liars, deceivers, and manipulators!!

[*Note – After fighting the war in Iraq for years, the U.S. outfitted the corrupt government leader of Iraq and "his people" with all kinds of military war machines, guns, and ammunition to continue the to fight terrorist groups. I am not so sure that we were not duped by that psychopath. Now we are fighting ISIS, who now has our military war machines, guns, and ammunitions.]

Remember that terrorists are psychopaths and will go "head-spinning ballistic" or "poltergeistic" when found out!!!! Someone who appears to be a charming client, friend, employee or confidant one minute may instantly turn out to be a two-faced hostile!!! Therefore, sometimes the best tactic is to not let the terrorists know that you are on to them!

All the lies and deception used by the ecoterrorists are usually just part of an elaborate crime scheme used to deprive their victims of their property; and, in the case of perverted charitable organizations, the lies and deception are used to fraudulently solicited donations!

Most animal communities have an alarm system to protect their group against the threat of predators; terrorists are predators. Sound the alarm. Don't be coerced, intimidated, or shamed by psychopaths. It is a fight against evil and injustice; so be relentless in seeking Justice. In the end, Truth and Justice will prevail.

Even if it kills me, I feel that it will leave the world a better place and God will reward me for it. I will be given another chance to be born again and take up the fight against Evil again in my next life; and, the terrorists, tyrants, and murders will be used as fuel for the fires of Hades!!!!

I sent out request for enunciation, correction, and retraction to some of those I thought to be duped accomplices; I was hoping to rescue a few of their souls; however, at times, I feel like it would better for the world if rather than trying to get them to repent, just let them go straight to Hell!!! In reality, even the duped accomplices; duped law enforcement; and, duped Justice System are either to embarrassed or cowardly to come forward to aid the victims.

Ecoterrorists like to run in packs and work undercover with a multitude of hidden agenda. So, it is extremely difficult to fight a vast network of ecoterrorists.

According one terrorist leader, "her people" had been undercover working for: Star Barn Thoroughbreds from the beginning; the Justice Department (state and/or federal); the Pennsylvania State Police; the Federal Bureau of Investigations; Penn National Gaming; the Nashville Metropolitan Health Department and/or the Tennessee Department of Health (medical director lady to be specific); People for the Ethical Treatment of Animals; the Humane Society of the United States; American Society for the Prevention of Cruelty to Animals; the New York Humane Society; and, a number of newspapers, magazines, horse publications and Broadcasting Companies.

When I bring this up, many do not believe it; however, actions - and sometimes inaction – speak louder than words. Law enforcement and the Justice System ignored my pleas for help; therefore, I now believe that this was a rare moment of truth for the terrorist leader.

> [*Many of the members of the crime group and/or duped accomplices have their own Thoroughbred operations. Many other perverted members of the crime group are masquerading as tax-exempt organizations with charitable causes.]

By creating and continually reinforcing the false impression that their targeted victims are sending horses to slaughter and starving and abusing horses; the members of the crime group who own Thoroughbred breeding and racing operations are deceitfully obtaining high-quality Thoroughbred horses at no cost - under the perverted color of official right; and, members of the crime group with perverted charities are fraudulently soliciting public donations for huge pecuniary gains.

The most despicable thing about the whole state of affairs is that rather than prosecuting the ecoterrorists and bringing them to justice, undercover and/or duped law enforcement officials, government officials, and officers of the Court are compounding the crimes and falsely prosecuting the victims and facilitating the theft of the horses and the fraudulent solicitation of charitable donations.

In our case, law enforcement has repeatedly investigated an outrageous number of false and fictitious reports; yet, law enforcement ignored my complaints of ecoterrorism, theft, and horses being harmed and killed.

Politically charged "perverted non-profit organizations" (posing as animal rights activists) have turned ecoterrorism into a lucrative art form!!!

Many politicians and world leaders have a problem wrapping their minds around the reality that terrorism of any kind is not about politics or religion. Terrorists only use religion and politics as covers to mask their despicable criminal activities. The fight against domestic or foreign terrorism is not a political or religious war; it is simply a fight between Good and Evil!!!

Any good philosopher, psychiatrist, or preacher will tell you – "the *evil in a thing will naturally destroy it*". So if you become a target - persevere!

Terrorist are nothing more than psychopaths – social parasites!! I will say it again and again – "terrorism is the darkest side of humanity"! It must be eradicated like a plague!

Any self-respecting duped accomplices would in my opinion turn states evidence against the terrorists and stop them from harming other targeted victims – both animal and human!!!

Perverted animal activists operate under the mask of non-profit organizations with noble causes; they often morph into well-organized crime groups, once they have duped law enforcement.

Ecoterrorists have an aberrant indifference to the plight of both their animal and human victims. Under the protection of their undercover law enforcement officials and political backers, they lack due respect and obedience to the law; they feel that laws and court orders are *"irrelevant"* - and do not apply to them. The lack of respect for the law is particularly obvious with corrupt government officials!

*Terroristic in-groups are often sophisticated and well-organized - and masked as a noble cause.

To psychopaths - "perception" is all that counts. Simply put - a psychopath losses touch with reality and the truth. Psychopathic behavior is often described as "humanity gone haywire". Ecoterrorism (and terrorism in general) is "politics and/or religion gone insane"!

Psychopathic in-groups learn how to masterfully create false impressions; and, how to continually reinforce the false impression – using a process called "parroting". Once they have the false impression thoroughly engrained in the minds of their "duped" accomplices and benefactors, they build off the false perceptions.

Ecoterrorists cannot comprehend the fact that animals and other human beings have rights. Many unexposed ecoterrorists are perceived as being animals lovers; however, the fact is *they have no capacity to love animals or other humans;* in fact, the animals and people they pretend to love are mere objects of their twisted crime schemes.

Terrorists usually *work on* their targeted victims by first constantly *degrading and/or vilifying* them. This is an integral part of all their crime schemes! They particularly like to project their despicable traits onto their victims. For example: Terrorists insanely justified the nine-eleven terrorist attacks by vilifying Christians. Same perverted thinking, just on a much larger scale than ecoterrorism!

Remember that the thing that psychopaths fears most is public exposure. This pulls back the veil that they have been hiding behind; however, in a society that accepts the moral low-road, psychopaths have an *extreme advantage* over the good, honest, trusting, and altruistic members of the society.

The Attorney General of PA, Kathleen Kane; the DA's in Lebanon, York, and Adams County; the FBI; the US Attorney General, Eric Holder; and, the PA Highway Patrol – all ignored my criminal complaints against the ecoterrorists.

A deadly disease that is allowed to spread untreated may wipeout an entire population!

Many corrupt government agencies aid and abet criminal activities by seizing healthy animals and falsely prosecuting the targeted owners. *This was a common practice in Nashville; it is a lucrative racket in PA.*

[*I know that I repeat things; however, like God and Mother Nature – I want to keep repeating key lessons over and over until the lessons are learned – so that others may benefit from the lessons that I have learned. Like my great-nephew encouraged the doctors to study his rare form of cancer in hope that they might find a cure; I encourage the readers to study my cancer (ecoterrorism) so that the world might find a cure for the despicable disease of terrorism.]

A real problem lies with undercover members of the corrupt organizations that have infiltrated law enforcement. For a democracy to survive, it must guard against giving tyrants, psychopaths, terrorists, and/or murders power and authority by ignoring their crimes!!!

Ecoterrorism is just a specialized form of terrorism used by veiled animal activists to exploit those who make their living participating in animal related activities.

The PA law entitled "Ecoterrorism" was enacted to protect two very basic human rights: the *"right to work"* in ones chosen line of work; and, the *"right to property"* – the right to own, use, enjoy, and benefit from one's personal property. How universally basic is that in a free world?"

The penalties for some of the crimes and offenses used by ecoterrorists to exploit their victims are: fines up to $250,000 or as much as double the pecuniary gain; up to 40 years imprisonment; and/or, treble the actual damages done to the victim.

These stiff mandated penalties should tell any sane person, that *ecoterrorism is a serious crime*; not a "civil or political feud"!!!! It's like telling someone who has been repeatedly beaten and robbed by a gang that it is a "civil" matter between him and the gang.

Nothing but death or incarceration will stop terrorism! After I had leased all the Trust horses to several different owners and trainers in a number of states, the ecoterrorists have hunted down, killed, harmed, maimed, and/or stolen most the Trust horses with the criminal intent to deprive me and the beneficiaries of the Trust of our tangible and intangible property.

The ecoterrorists have never had any legal right or privilege to deprive me or the beneficiaries of the Trust of our property. *All that they really have is a "sick sense of entitlement" – sarcastically speaking - after all they did put countless woman-hours into their efforts to sabotage and to put SBT out of business so that they could get their hands on the horses.*

[Yes you read it right. Except for a few *duped and used* male accomplices, the terrorists group that targeted Dr. Barr and me is made up of primarily women; women who seem to be *gender-biased.* Even their coconspirator from Nashville is referred to as the "medical director lady".]

The crime group had absolutely no right to take the Trust horses; they had absolutely no privilege to infringe on all the Trust's different business relations; and, they have absolutely no legitimate interest in the Trust's property – tangible or intangible.

As a matter of law, the ecoterrorists and their undercover accomplices in law enforcement and the Justice System are nothing but criminals and racketeers!!!!!!!!!!!!!!

PA Title 18 Chapter 39 § 3901: Definitions. **"Property of another"** - *Includes property in which* **any person other than the actor has an interest which the actor is not privileged to infringe,** *regardless of the fact that the actor also has an interest in the property and regardless of the fact that the other person might be precluded from civil recovery because the property was used in an unlawful transaction or was subject to forfeiture as contraband.*

Even if the ecoterrorists had successfully framed me, they still have no right or justifications for stealing the Trust horses and depriving the beneficiaries of the Trust of their tangible and intangible property: contract rights; horses; stallion awards; breeder's awards; track earnings; owner's awards; etc.

PA Title 18 Chapter 39 § 3921: **Theft by unlawful taking or disposition.** *(a) Movable property.--A person is guilty of theft if he unlawfully takes, or exercises unlawful control over, movable property of another with intent to deprive him thereof.*

All the ecoterrorists who have any of the stolen horses are criminals!!!!!!!!!!!!!!!!

Even Orders of the Court did not stop these ecoterrorist. According to Deb Jones, Orders of the Court are "irrelevant"!

PA Title 18 Chapter 39 § 3922: **Theft by deception.** *(a) Offense defined.--A person is guilty of theft if he intentionally obtains or withholds property of another by deception. A person deceives if he intentionally:*

(1) **Creates or reinforces a false impression,** *including false impressions as to law, value, intention or other state of mind;*

(2) **Prevents another from acquiring information which would affect his judgment of a transaction;** *or,*

(3) **Fails to correct a false impression which the deceiver previously created or reinforced, or which the deceiver knows to be influencing another to whom he stands in a fiduciary or confidential relationship.** *PA Title 18 Chapter 39 § 3923:* **Theft by extortion.** *(a) Offense defined.--A person is guilty of theft if he intentionally obtains or withholds property of another by threatening to:*

(1) **Commit another criminal offense;**

(2) **accuse anyone of a criminal offense;**

(3) *expose any secret tending to* **subject any person to hatred, contempt or ridicule;**

(4) **take or withhold action as an official,** *or* **cause an official to take or withhold action;**

(5) *bring about or continue a strike,* **boycott** *or other* **collective unofficial action, if the property is not demanded or received for the benefit of the group in whose interest the actor purports to act;**

(6) **testify or provide information or withhold testimony or information with respect to the legal claim or defense of another;** *or*

(7) **inflict any other harm which would not benefit the actor.** *PA Title 18 Chapter 39 § 3925:* **Receiving stolen property.**

(a) *Offense defined.--A person is guilty of theft if he* **intentionally receives, retains, or disposes of movable property of another knowing that it has been stolen, or believing that it has probably been stolen,** *unless the property is received, retained, or disposed with intent to restore it to the owner.*

(b) *Definition.--As used in this section the word* **"receiving" means acquiring possession, control or title,** *or lending on the security of the property.*

As the article in the *Pennsylvania Equestrian* points out - The "Get Rich" signature crime scheme of the terrorists *has* caused the death of dozens of stolen horses – only the ecoterrorists would know the fate of the horses stolen from the Trust. They obviously continue to fight amongst themselves over the stolen horses!!

> *Why were the Trust horses killed? The "why" is obvious: and, I quote the ecoterrorists – "you couldn't run a dead horse" and "good news for you Paul E. Truitt none of these horses will ever run" and "they are all going to die". And dead horses are of considerable value to the ecoterrorists to create "shock value" which is expertly used to fraudulently raise donations.*

> *The whole "Star Barn Saga" and the "Star Barn Carnage" is a psychopathic scam and very similar to the Ohio scam involving "52 horses going to slaughter on Saturday".*

> *The "Ohio Scam" successfully brought in "Urgent" donations for over two years after the owner and his family had already placed the horses in new homes and the owner had passed away.*

Now after almost three years since Star Barn was force out of business by these ecoterrorists, the psychopathic "Star Barn Scam" is still going strong and fraudulently soliciting donations to care for and to train "stolen" Trust horses.

> *The entire Facebook page "Star Barn Thoroughbreds – Broodmares in Urgent Need of Placement" is nothing more than a scam: to fraudulently raise donation; and, to orchestrate the rest of this continuing criminal conspiracy!*

The Facebook page is self-incriminating to many of the ecoterrorists. When law enforcement starts looking for coconspirators, all they will have to do is go to the website - and to published and broadcasted news - to identify the players in this well-orchestrated and well-publicized criminal conspiracy.

These psychopathic ecoterrorists, masquerading as animal activists, need to be *"Urgently Placed"* in prison so that they will stop harming, stealing, and killing horses to create *"shock value"* and using the fabricated *"shock value"* to con real animal lovers into making donations that only benefits the narcissistic ring leaders.

The organized crime group in PA also claims to have people working undercover for them in law enforcement; in the News Media; in the Justice System; and, at the race track. This problem needs to be "Urgently" addressed by the PA Attorney General, Kathleen Kane; or, someone who knows that they have *"oversight"* over corrupt organizations in that state.

Because the Office of the Attorney General is ignorant of the fact that it does have the power and duty to investigate and prosecute corrupt organizations, I would not recommend Pennsylvania as a place to try to conduct business of any kind; especially, the infiltrated and targeted Thoroughbred industry in that state. As often depicted in movies based on true stories, PA has more than its share of psychopaths and corrupt organizations; and, they are ignored by law enforcement that could and should do something to protect the victims - and the victims' property.

> *If the truth was known, Pennsylvania would probably be at the top of "The 10 most corrupt states in the U.S." - mostly because PA lets terrorists from several other states come in and infiltrate its law enforcement and legitimate businesses; and, to usurp the power and authority of its Justice System.*

Any Thoroughbred owner or trainer going to PA is stepping into a *terrorist trap*; and, will experience *the darkest side of Thoroughbred racing.* They run the risk of the ecoterrorists tampering with their horses; especially, the ones entered to race.

> *Prior to racing and training at Penn National, my horses were being tranquilized and tampered with by undercover ecoterrorists. I understand that the ecoterrorists are now demanding that felony charges be brought against trainers who horses test positive. How scary is that? The undercover ecoterrorists working for the trainer dope the trainer's horse and then demand that the trainer be charged with a felony, since their horse tested positive.*

The estimated damages to the Trust; its beneficiaries; and, me amount to over $40 million. The collateral damage done by the ecoterrorist is catastrophic. In the Commonwealth of Pennsylvania, the victim's road to Justice is blocked by: psychopathic ecoterrorists; duped accomplices; undercover law enforcement; undercover track officials; and, a corrupt Justice System.

> *The outrageous assault on the good and honest citizens of PA needs to be addressed by the PA Attorney General. Although she denies that she has the oversight; as a matter of law, she does have the power and duty to investigate and prosecute alleged corrupt organizations.*

Three times I filed complaints about this corrupt organization with the Office of the Attorney General of the Commonwealth of Pennsylvania. All three times I was told that it was a civil matter and that I need to get a civil attorney. The first two times, I was told that no crimes had been committed. The last time, I was told that the Office of the Attorney General has no oversight on matters alleging corrupt organizations.

Because it is obviously a criminal matter, I cannot get a civil litigator to take the case. Or like my former attorney in Adams County, maybe the Attorney General's Office all of a sudden has a conflict of interest.

I cannot blame a civil attorney for not wanting to take on corrupt government. This is also a big problem in the # 3 Most Corrupt State - Tennessee; government officials there were either corrupt or they were ignorant of their own laws; and, civil attorneys would not touch anything that had to do with corrupt government.

[* Note - The Attorney General of PA certainly does not have the "insight" to do something about the corruption in her state; even though, the PA criminal statutes clearly state that she has the "oversight", duty and obligation to do so.]

PA Title 18 Chapter 9 § 911: **Corrupt organizations**; (a) Findings of fact.--The General Assembly finds that:

(1) organized crime is a highly sophisticated, diversified, and widespread phenomenon which annually **drains billions of dollars from the national economy** by various **patterns of unlawful conduct** including the illegal use of force, fraud, and corruption;

(2) **Organized crime exists on a large scale within the Commonwealth of Pennsylvania**, engaging in the same patterns of unlawful conduct which characterize its activities nationally;

(3) the vast amounts of money and power accumulated by organized crime are increasingly **used to infiltrate and corrupt legitimate businesses** operating within the Commonwealth, together with all of the **techniques of violence, intimidation**, and other **forms of unlawful conduct through which such money and power are derived**;

(4) in furtherance of such infiltration and corruption, **organized crime utilizes and applies to its unlawful purposes laws of the Commonwealth of Pennsylvania** conferring and relating to the privilege of engaging in various types of business and designed to insure that such businesses are conducted in furtherance of the public interest and the general economic welfare of the Commonwealth;

*(5) such infiltration and corruption provide an outlet for illegally obtained capital, harm innocent investors, entrepreneurs, merchants and consumers, **interfere with free competition,** and thereby **constitute a substantial danger to the economic and general welfare of the Commonwealth of Pennsylvania**; and*

*(6) in order to successfully resist and eliminate this situation, it is necessary to provide **new remedies and procedures.***

*(e) **Enforcement.** –*

*(1) The **Attorney General** shall have the **power and duty to enforce** the provisions of this section, including the authority to issue civil investigative demands pursuant to subsection (f), institute proceedings under subsection (d), and to take such actions as may be necessary to ascertain and investigate alleged violations of this section.*

*(2) The **Attorney General** and the **district attorneys** of the several counties shall have concurrent authority to institute criminal proceedings under the provisions of this section.*

(3) Nothing contained in this subsection shall be construed to limit the regulatory or investigative authority of any department or agency of the Commonwealth whose functions might relate to persons, enterprises, or matters falling within the scope of this section.

*PA Title 18 Chapter 51 § 5111: **Dealing in proceeds of unlawful activities;***

*(a) Offense defined.--A person commits **a felony of the first degree** if the person conducts a financial transaction under any of the following circumstances:*

*(1) With knowledge that **the property involved,** including **stolen or illegally obtained property,** represents the proceeds of unlawful activity, the person acts with the **intent to promote the carrying on of the unlawful activity.***

*(2) With knowledge that **the property involved,** including **stolen or illegally obtained property,** represents the proceeds of unlawful activity and that **the transaction is designed in whole or in part to conceal or disguise the nature, location, source, ownership or control of the proceeds of unlawful activity.***

*(3) **To avoid a transaction reporting requirement under State or Federal law.***

*(b) Penalty.--Upon conviction of a violation under subsection (a), a person shall be sentenced to **a fine of the greater of $100,000 or twice the value of the property involved in the transaction or to imprisonment for not more than 20 years, or both.***

(c) *Civil penalty.--A person who conducts or attempts to conduct a transaction described in subsection (a) is liable to the Commonwealth for a civil penalty of the greater of:*

(1) **The value of the property, funds or monetary instruments involved in the transaction;**

(d) *Cumulative remedies.--Any proceedings under this section* **shall be in addition to any other criminal penalties or forfeitures authorized under the State law.**

(e) **Enforcement.** –

(1) *The* **Attorney General** *shall have the* **power and duty** *to institute proceedings to recover the civil penalty provided under subsection (c) against any person liable to the Commonwealth for such a penalty.*
Ecoterrorism *is a serious crime. (Only a few crimes such as capital murder carry stiffer penalties.) The penalty for committing* **the crime of ecoterrorism and related crimes against property is up to 40 years imprisonment and a fine of up to $250,000.**
The statutory restitution due the victims of ecoterrorism is up to three times the actual damages.

Since PA is such a corrupt state, the probable outcome to "The Star Barn Scam" is that the fraudulent and coercive practices of the ecoterrorists will simply be *ignored and go unpunished*. Rather than prosecuting the ecoterrorists and collecting the fines for the egregious crimes that were committed; *the victims of the ecoterrorism and the citizens PA will be the only ones that are punished.*

> *I would suggest that victims of organized crime in PA or TN move to a more business friendly state. I know I let out a big yell of relief when I crossed the state line leaving Pennsylvania.*

> *However, much to my chagrin, like the Nashville crime group beat me to PA; their PA coconspirators beat me to KY and had already devised a con to take the rest of the Trust horses!*

CHAPTER 24

Requests for Enunciation
and Correction

Because I was naïve enough to believe that at least one or two of the ecoterrorists would have a conscience, I send out requests for correction, retraction, and enunciation to several of them. I thought my request would separate the true sociopaths from the duped accomplices. Only one responded and she was flabbergasted that I even suspected her, even though she was in the middle of the Adams County SPCA scandal. The rest just retreated back under their rocks. Like the vipers they are, I suspect they will camouflage themselves and strike again when least expected.

> I requested that members of the Facebook page – "Star Barn Thoroughbreds - Broodmares Need Urgent Placement" (and participating members of the media) to correct and retract all of the false and malicious statements publicized or said about me and my business relations.

> I also requested that those members of the group with a conscience and/or were "duped" into participating in the fraudulent and coercive practices of the group - contact their local law enforcement and renunciate their roles in this criminal conspiracy.

I was even naïve enough to think that my rights - and the rights of my innocent beneficiaries - would be protected by law enforcement and the Justice System. I send out several complaints to numerous law enforcement agencies – local, state and federal. This was also futile! I even sent my story to major newspapers and television networks – absolutely no response! I even was naïve enough to believe that the Pennsylvania Equestrian would retract and correct the despicable story they printed in June of 2014.

I have reported the horses taken from Star Barn Thoroughbred Breeders' Trust-A by members the crime group as stolen. So if a member of the group has one of these stolen horses, do not try to sell these stolen properties – selling stolen property and ecoterrorism are classified as first class felonies with a penalty of up to 40 years in prison and a fine no more than $100,000. Selling stolen property may carry a fine of up to $250,000.

Furthermore, depriving the innocent beneficiaries of Star Barn Thoroughbred Breeders Trust–A of their property is insane and despicable!!!!!

If anyone has one of the Trust horses; made fraudulently solicited or coerced donations to the group; or was duped into aiding this group in any way, please contact law enforcement in your county and state and in Lebanon, County, PA.

CONCLUSION

The world is made up of good and evil; caretakers and takers; those that build and those that destroy. Terrorists (domestic or foreign) are evil people with evil motives; often masquerading as political activists with a noble political or religious cause. In reality, the primary objective is personal gain. The fight against terrorism (domestic or foreign) is not really a fight between people with different religious beliefs or political views; it is simply a fight between Good and Evil.

Terrorists are predators. They capitalize on a phenomenon of nature called "naïve prey syndrome". This is where the prey does not recognized their enemies until it is too late. Terrorism is so successful because: terrorists play by no rules; have no moral values; and, they have no conscience or sense of remorse! Depriving their victims of their lives, freedom, and/or property brings the terrorists a depraved sense of accomplishment and perverted pleasure.

In reality, terrorists (domestic or foreign) do not have the capacity to love - people or animals; people and animals are merely objects used by terrorists for personal gain and pleasure.

> *There was absolutely no reason or justification for the terrorists to harm the Trust horses or to attack our Charitable Trust and deprive its helpless beneficiaries of their tangible and intangible property.*

True to their psychopathic character, the ecoterrorists maliciously sought out and systematically destroyed *"all"* the Trust's business relations; more egregiously, they killed and stole the very horses that would have benefited the donors and beneficiaries that the crime group insanely claimed had been defrauded. Furthermore, they despicably took property and benefits from three charities that benefit critically ill children!

Without any right or justification, it took the ecoterrorists two years to put Star Barn Thoroughbreds at Agrarian Country out of business; it took the well-organized crime group another three years to deprive the Charitable Trust of all its assets. The beneficiaries of the Charitable Trust were the only ones that had a legal right to benefit from, and not be deprived of, the tangible and intangible property of the Trust: including, the horses, the contracts rights, the track earnings, and the lucrative PA Breeders, Owners, and Stallion awards. There was absolutely no way for the ecoterrorists to spin this; yet law enforcement quietly let the terrorists get away with elaborate crime schemes!

Fighting psychopaths and terrorists is like playing in a sport where one team must plays by the rules; and, the other team makes up their own rules!

The terrorists insanely carried out their published threats; while law enforcement ignored their despicable crimes.

Ecoterrorists have developed sophisticated ways to harm and kill animals; ways that will go undetected and uninvestigated; but, reflect badly on the targeted owners and trainers!

"You couldn't run a dead horse" is one of the anti- racing ecoterrorists' sinister sayings. As I have been so painfully made aware off!

The most despicable thing about the Justice System in TN and PA is that rather than prosecuting the domestic terrorists and bringing them to justice, undercover and/or duped law enforcement officials, government officials, and officers of the Court compound the terroristic crimes by falsely prosecuting the victims; thus, facilitating the theft of the livestock and the fraudulent solicitation of charitable donations.

Lists of Dead, Missing and Stolen Trust Horses

Horses Taken by Coconspirators in Adams County

11-A filly Named Jilly	ch f	Snow Ridge G1 711k
11-Cat ID	db/br c	Jockey's Dream G1 E114
11-Deealta	ch c	Snow Ridge G1 711k
11-Express Lover	db/br f	It's So Simple 108 388k E113
11-Full Body Girl	b c	Snow Ridge G1 711k
11-Hey Doll	DEAD	Senor Swinger G2 964k

11-Malibu Express	b f	Ecclesiastic G3 346k
11-Maydeuce	db/br c	Snow Ridge G1 711k
11-My Lucky Number	ch c	Ecclesiastic G3 346k
11-Polly Lynch	db/br f	Jockey's Dream G1 E114
11-Prize Possession	db/br f	It's So Simple 108 388k E113
11-Rex's Best 157k	ch f	Snow Ridge G1 711k
11-Romper Room	ch f	Snow Ridge G1 711k
11-Serval	ch f	Snow Ridge G1 711k
11-The Katy	ch c	Snow Ridge G1 711k
11-Walk Your Talk	db/gr c	Senor Swinger G2 964k
11-Wired For Success	DEAD	It's So Simple 108 388k E113

Other Dead, Missing and/or Stolen 2011 Foals

11-California Love	db/br c	Ecclesiastic G3 346k
11-Get Up 1sw	b f	It's So Simple 108 388k E113
11-Kegtown	db/br c	Jockey's Dream G1 E114
11-Lady Brahms	ch c	It's So Simple 108 388k E113
11-Minstrel's Gold	b f	It's So Simple 108 388k E113
11-Miss Lady Randolph	DEAD	It's So Simple 108 388k E113
11-Newquay	DEAD	Snow Ridge G1 711k
11-Opening Speech	b f	Snow Ridge G1 711k
11-Pete n' Pete	DEAD	Senor Swinger G2 964k
11-Static Discharge	DEAD	Jockey's Dream G1 E114
11-Stormy Danyelle	ch f	Snow Ridge G1 711k
11-Sugar Doll	DEAD	Snow Ridge G1 711k

Dead and Stolen Stallions: Victims of Ecoterrorism

Jockey's Dream G1 E114	DEAD	Spend A Buck HOY KD 4.2M
Classic Romeo	2006 ch h	Essence of Dubai G2 2M

Dead, Stolen and/or Missing Broodmares

Pete N' Pete	db/br m	A.P. Indy BS BCC HOY 2LS 3M
Tejano Music	gr m	Ferdinand HOY 3.8M KD BCC
The Katy w	db/br m	Cryptoclearance G1 BS 3.4M
Hey Doll w	gr m	Siphon G1 3M
Prize Possession 58k	ch m	Prized G1 BCT 2.6 M
Example w	ch m	Touch Gold G1 BS 1.7M
Serval	ch m	Lord Carson G2 ntr 655k
Colonial Ball sp	b m	Pleasant Colony CH KD PS 965k
Malek's Jewel	ch m	Malek (Chi) CH 2M
Sweet Anna	b f	Essence of Dubai G2 2M
Silver Sceptre	gr m	Urgent Request (Ire) G1 1.2 M
Walk Your Talk 46k	db/br m	Talkin Man CH 678k
Lucina	db/br m	Benchmark G2
Malibu Express	db/br m	Malibu Moon LS 34k
Stormy Sunshine	gr m	Future Storm G3 338k
Wired for Success	b m	Catienus SW 370k
Hyacinths of Gold	b m	Bartok (Ire)SW
Lady Brahms	db/br m	Brahms G1 843k
Jump Lightly	db/br m	Jump Start G2 221k
Deealta	ch m	Twining G2 238k
Personal Joy	db/br m	Personal Flag G1 1.3M
Rex's Best	b m	Rex Imperator G3 187k
Maydeuce	db/br m	Deputed Testamony G1 PS 674k
Lady of Interest	db/br f	Changeintheweather G1 441k
Minstrel's Gold	ch f	Reba's Gold G3 .7M
Polly Lynch	db/br m	Our Emblem G1pl 366k
Romper Room	b m	Deposit Ticket G1 444k
Full Body Girl	db/br f	Full Mandate SW 193k
May Day Dancer	b m	Eavesdropper SW 168k
Devine By Design w	ch m	Poteen SW 436K
Tokenness	ch m	Count the Time G3 677k

Miss Lady Randolph	ch m	Center Cut SW 249k
On Top	ch f	Old Topper G3 656k
Weekend Miesque	b f	Eavesdropper SW 168k
California Love	DEAD	Strawberry Road CH HOY 1.7M 3C
Sarah's Girl	DEAD	Lost Code G1 (2) 2M
My Lucky Number	DEAD	Polish Number sp 80k
Kegtown	DEAD	Capetown G1 795k

Dead or Missing 2012, 2013 & 2014 Foals

12-Colonial Ball	DEAD	It's So Simple 388k E113
12-Deealta	foal	Jockey's Dream G1 E114
12-Devine by Design	foal	Jockey's Dream G1 E114
12-Example	foal	Jockey's Dream G1 E114
12-Full Body Girl	foal	Jockey's Dream G1 E114
12-Hey Doll	foal	Jockey's Dream G1 E114
12-Hyacinths of Gold	foal	Jockey's Dream G1 E114
12-Lucina	foal	Jockey's Dream G1 E114
12-Jump Lightly	foal	Jockey's Dream G1 E114
12-Malek's Jewel	foal	Jockey's Dream G1 E114
12-Malibu Express	foal	It's So Simple 388k E113
12-Maydeuce	foal	Jockey's Dream G1 E114
12-Minstrel's Gold	foal	Jockey's Dream G1 E114
12-Personal Joy	foal	Jockey's Dream G1 E114
12-Pete n' Pete	foal	Jockey's Dream G1 E114
12-Polly Lynch	foal	Jockey's Dream G1 E114
12-Romper Room	foal	Jockey's Dream G1 E114
12-Prize Possession	foal	Jockey's Dream G1 E114
12-Rex's Best 157k	foal	It's So Simple 388k E113
12-Serval	foal	Jockey's Dream G1 E114
12-Silver Sceptre	foal	Jockey's Dream G1 E114
12-Stormy Sunshine	foal	It's So Simple 388k E113
12- Sweet Anna	foal	Jockey's Dream G1 E114

12-Tejano Music	foal	Jockey's Dream G1 E114
12-The Katy	foal	Jockey's Dream G1 E114
12-Tokenness	foal	Jockey's Dream G1 E114
12-Wake Up Maggie BB	DEAD	Jockey's Dream G1 E114
12-Walk Your Talk	foal	Jockey's Dream G1 E114
12-Wired For Success	foal	Jockey's Dream G1 E114

Post Script

As of October of 2014 "The Star Barn Scam" was still active:

"The Star Barn Saga" was over on Oct. 28, 2011; before and since that time, dozens of stolen Trust horses have died cruel deaths at the hands of the ecoterrorists.

How twisted is the account of the death of the darted weanling in the June 2014 Amy Worden's article, "The Star Barn Saga: 'Get Rich' Scheme Costs Dozens of Horses' Lives"? "One dart lodged in the filly's intestine was not removed. She died ten days later." *This is insane, ignorant, and cruel.* It takes a cruel and deranged person to shot an animal in their gut; intentionally leave the dart in the intestine; and, let the animal suffer for 10 long days before they die of peritonitis – and *then to insanely claim that the death was due to "parasites and starvation".* This shows how ignorant and cruel the terrorists are; and, how out of touch with Reality they are.

Furthermore, how insane is it to state that the despicably death of a 9 month-old-horse that could have never been owned by SBT (and caused by the negligence of alleged "authorities") become part of the "Star Barn Carnage"? Can't anyone but me see through this despicable scam? Can anyone but me see just how insane these people are? *Maybe you have to be one of the victims to see just how evil domestic terrorists are* – as many of the duped accomplices have, or will, find out.

Even the duped *undercover law enforcement and Justice System officials are probably going to be targeted by the ecoterrorists* when their usefulness plays out. There will come a time when the terrorists will want to silence their duped accomplices; especially, those in *law enforcement.* Remember that *terrorists play by their own rules!*

It is believed that several of the 2011, 2012, 2013, and 2014 Trust foals were intentionally taken and destroyed by the ecoterrorist in-group simply because one of the group's insane objectives is to make sure that Paul E. Truitt will not make any money off any of these horses; by insanely making sure that none of the Trust's horses are ever raced.

As some of the perverted "rescuers" say, "You couldn't run a dead horse."

A picture of Jockey's Dream is on the cover of this book. This picture was taken at Star Barn Thoroughbreds before he was taken by theft by deception. I have heard three totally different accounts of the *multiple deaths* of **Jockey's Dream** from the ecoterrorists:

*(1) Debbi Rogers first informed me of his alleged death on **Nov. 14, 2012** (and I quote) "the f*****g horse is lying dead in a field". Her coconspirators also posted on their Facebook page around that time, "RIP Jockey's Dream" - as they celebrated his alleged death.*

*(2) On or around **March 2014**, according to Debbi Rogers a "headless" Jockey's Dream was found by Rogers and Calhoun on another farm in MD. Rogers failed to call me this time.*

(3) In July of 2014, coconspirator Houseman informed me that Jockey's Dream died at New Bolton Center.

In 2012, according to Houseman and Rogers, they had a buyer *that wanted to move Jockey's Dream to Australian, to replace his full bother, Champion Investor's Dream who had just died.*

[*I often wonder if the psychopaths had planned to send me his "missing" head, because I would not turn him over to them.]

Jockey's Dream was never owned by Star Barn Thoroughbreds. In 2012, Houseman took Jockey's Dream by theft by deception and refused to return the stallion.

Back in November of 2012, when Houseman would not turn Jockey's Dream and all the other horses over to Rogers, she went "ballistic" and told me that Jockey's Dream was dead. And because Houseman would not let her know where the rest of the horse were that *"they are all going die"*. When I called Houseman, he told me that the group had mistaken another black stallion for Jockey's Dream *(one that he had helped Jones rescue from New Holland)* while Jockey's Dream was babysitting the weanlings in a nearby field.

One of the characteristics of psychopaths is that they are master liars and manipulators. After a while, you cannot believe a word psychopaths say; so subject everything they say to close scrutiny. After a while it becomes apparent just how evil and insane they are.

Take Rogers for instance - On **Nov. 14, 2012**, when I could not tell her were the stolen Trust horses were (because I did not know), *Rogers went head-spinning "ballistic" (like she did again in 2014 when they told her Jockey's Dream was dead - again). After she charmingly tried to find out if I knew where Houseman was keeping Jockey's Dream and the other horses, I told her that I knew what she was up to. When she figured out that I was on to her, Roger's then went ballistic and said,* **"I want you to know that the f*****g horses is lying dead in a field"**; *that the rest of the horses were going to die; and, then she ended the conversation with "you are a "mother f****r" and I hope you rot in hell."*

> *Then sometime after* **March of 2014** *– It was published in the Pennsylvania Equestrian that "Jockey's Dream was the one that sent me over the edge," said Rogers, who had tried to get Houseman to turn over the stallion to her. "The day my mother died,* **they told me the stallion was dead**. *I was ballistic."*
>
> *– June 2014 Pennsylvania Equestrian – The News Horse Owners Need to Know*

Didn't Rogers just say in the previous paragraph of that article that **she and Calhoun found the headless body of Jockey's Dream**? Why would "they" have to tell her that he was dead *yet again* in the next paragraph of the "The Star Barn Saga" article?

How could anyone identify him when his head was his distinguishing feature? Other than a small star, he had no markings. *How does one age the remains of a horse with no head – and no tattoo? Only those that "beheaded" Jockey's Dream would know that the headless body belonged to him.*

And who was the previous owner who allegedly identified him? It certainly was not me. Was it Houseman? He never owned the horse. Or was it actual a previous owner that they were trying to "shame" into making a donation?

Law enforcement needs to start taking DNA samples to identify the dead horses. And when I say law enforcement, I don't mean Jones, Rogers, and/or their "authorities". I for one would like to know where all the stolen Trust horses have gone; and, if they are in fact dead!!

Rogers had been after Jockey's Dream for a couple of year. Obviously Jockey's Dream was her *"secret reward"* for playing her role in the *continuing criminal conspiracy*. Since the times that the ecoterrorists attempted to extort the horses from Dr. Barr back in 2011, they have had a pathological sense of entitlement to the Trust and SBT horses. *Obviously, Rogers felt entitled to Jockey's Dream, just because she allegedly had a home and/or buyer for this stolen Trust horse.*

Finally, Jockey's Dream was *never owned by Star Barn Thoroughbreds* as stated in the article. Jockey's Dream was given to me and I donated him to the Trust.

Then he was later taken by theft by deception by undercover coconspirator, Houseman – most probably to placate his coconspirators, Jones and Rogers!!

[*Note – Jockey's Dream was a multiple graded stakes winner by Spend a Buck (Horse of the Year; World Record earner of over $4 million; and, winner of the Kentucky Derby a few days before his third birthday). Jockey's Dream was also the full brother of Champion Investor's Dream.

Jockey's Dream and his babies held a very special place in my heart. Back in the late 70's, I started a Bloodstock Agency. My first client was Rowe Harper the breeder of Spend a Buck. I selected a mare, named Belle de Jour, for Mr. Harper out of a public auction. Mr. Harper purchased her for $18,000. I later recommended that Mr. Harper breed Belle de Jour to Buckaroo. That mating produced Spend a Buck.]

I asked *PENNSYLVANIA EQUESTRIAN* to Retract and Correction the defamatory article and got no response!

ABOUT THE AUTHOR

The author spent most of his life caring for the health, safety and welfare of animals of all kinds. He grew up on an award winning livestock farm near Stanley, KY with seven siblings.

While growing up, the author received a number of student achieve and athletic awards. After graduating from Auburn University's School of Veterinary Medicine, he was later considered by his colleagues to be one of the best veterinary surgeons in Tennessee. And in the 1980's, the author was one of most success Thoroughbred horse trainers and bloodstock agents in America.

During his mid-life crises, the author intensely studied: Business; Education; Psychology; Philosophy; Logic; Interpersonal Relationship; Communication; and, Comparative Religion.

As a college instructor, Dr. Truitt taught *"Biology – The Nature of Life"* and *"Human Health and Biology"*. As a single parent's leader, he gave lectures on "Interpersonal Relationships", "Love and Friendship", "Forgiveness", and "Innate Human Needs". Dr. Truitt also facilitated faith-based courses on single parenting.

Dr. Truitt has been employed by government agencies on four different occasions; however, his work ethic, honesty, and integrity did not mix well with two of these agencies. Because of his willingness to stand up for what was right, conflicts were unavoidable. For the past decade and a half, Dr. Truitt has been continuously targeted by corrupt government officials and ecoterrorists masquerading as animal activists and charitable organizations.

Because of his extended veterinary medical background and education: in Management of Non-Profit Organizations and Metro Government Management; organizing and operating a NPO, Animal Health Safety and Welfare, Inc.; working with other legitimate non-profit organizations; and, years working with animal related law enforcement – Dr. Truitt was able to recognized the well-masked crime schemes use by his government employed enemies and the ecoterrorists – and the government cover-ups that followed.

Although Dr. Truitt lost his home, farm, and livelihood: he still stood up for what is right and good. He still believes that his primary purpose in this life is to fight his divinely allotted battles against evil forces in our world.

Reward Offered

REWARD – A maximum reward of 10% of a Court Ordered and Collected Settlement.

Estimated Actual Damages: $41.35million
Estimated Statutory Damages: $124.05 million
Estimated Punitive Damages: $413.5 million
Requested Damages: $578.9 million

CONDITIONS of REWARD – Dr. Truitt is offering a reward which will be proportionately divided among any and all persons (including, unindicted coconspirators; private investigators; duped government officials; duped donors and benefactors; duped accomplices; charitable organizations; and, private concerned citizens) who play a willful and relevant role in bringing members of this crime group and corrupt government officials to Justice and successfully help make Star Barn Thoroughbred Breeders' Trust-A "whole".

Actual estimated damages to the Charitable Trust and Paul E. Truitt are estimated to be close to $40 million. Statutory damages for ecoterrorism are treble that amount. And due the despicable and vicious nature of the terroristic acts – the punitive damages should be several times that amount.

Any legal advocates who are willing to litigate the case on a contingency basis will also be compensated at the rate of 40% of the final collected court ordered settlement. The statutes of limitations will run out in October of 2016 if no more overt acts are committed by any of the coconspirators in this continuing criminal conspiracy. Therefore, the contingent offer will also expire in October of 2016.

Final Reward Contracts Must Be In Writing Along With Signed Affidavits of Pertinent Knowledge of the Crimes!

CPSIA information can be obtained at www.ICGtesting.com
Printed in the USA
LVOW11s1734010315

428825LV00001B/309/P